THE HARVEST

Service Driven Sales in a Me Driven World

Lori Borre

For information about speaking engagements or to host a book signing, contact Lori@loriborre.com with "Events" in the subject line.

Front cover photography by William Borre

ISBN 978-1-952281-50-1 (paperback edition)
ISBN 978-1-952281-49-5 (eBook edition)

Foreword

One of Zig Ziglar's most favorite quotes is, "You can have everything in life you want if you will just help other people to get what they want." Lori Borre has delivered this outcome with her practical insights through life experiences and a real desire to help and be of service. Mary Young defines a leader by how they make others feel. By sharing her personal vulnerabilities, Lori guides us to awaken, own, and identify how we each possess a creative agency to determine and reshape our lives through mastering the skill of listening, asking questions, and most importantly closing. One of the most valuable skills in the world today is simply the ability to sell our ideas, beliefs, services, and even products. In any organization or business in every country in the world, power moves inexorably to those who are persuasive! What is important is that you have a way to convince, persuade, and come into alignment with our friends, family, colleagues, customers, investors, etc. that your ideas are worthwhile. Over the years, I've identified some fundamentals to the art of selling and closing. Lori addresses these fundamentals and makes them simple to understand and execute. I love how she expresses that the customer must always be the one who gets the better end of the deal. Being of service while creating relationships is what this all comes down to! Loving what you are doing plays a major role for us as Lori demonstrates how easy it is to start a conversation with anybody, especially Uber drivers! I am honored to have ignited her passion to writing this book and sharing what seems so simple for her with all of us. This little book is a masterful education in how to play the long game in building success in your Young Living® business. To build and create success you must have 4 components: integrity, intelligence, experience, and dedication. Lori shares all four with us through her words and passion.

Marcella Vonn Harting, PhD

Young Living® Essential Oils, Royal Crown Diamond

All My Rowdy Friends
(Acknowledgments)

My Husband Ron and the Borre Boys

To the love of my life, my heart and my soul. Little did you know what you were getting into 35 years ago when you asked for my hand. Thank you for loving me and trusting my judgment, even when others called me "Crazy Lori," and thank you for loving your children enough to never question the cost of true health. Your support has meant the world to me, and it has allowed me to fly. You are such a strong, courageous, faithful man, and if I might say so too, my kinda hot tamale. I'm pretty sure I married up. I am so excited to see where the next 35 years together takes us.

To the boys who made me a mom. You are the reason I am so passionate about natural childbirth, home birth, and nursing. You are the reason I have fought so hard to protect the rights of others. You are the reason I am so passionate about educating others about natural wellness. All of you made me a warrior mom. I couldn't have asked for better kids, and I am so proud of the men you are becoming. You are going to do great things in your lives. As you continue the legacy, may the Lord surround you with truly good people, for each of you is so easy to love, and may you stand on our shoulders and see further than we can see.

Marcella Vonn Harting

I will always remember the first time I saw you. I drove 5 hours to a meeting where I sat front-row-center, wearing my yellow dress, and taking copious notes. That Senior Star decided then and there that she would do as you had done. Truly, I can trace so much of what I do to what I learned that pivotal day.

Sharing the stage with you at James and Stacy's IMPACT event was a dream I never would have believed could happen. My heart started pounding, and I broke out in a cold sweat when you looked me in the eye, and charged me to write a book on what I had just taught. With an audience full of witnesses, how could I deny your challenge? That day, you taught me how to do it scared and not play it safe. You saw me. You still see me.

There is no way I could fit everything I've learned from you over the years into these few paragraphs, but I hope the examples throughout this book will introduce others to your sage advice. Thank you for believing in and for embodying the spirit of Young Living®. Thank you for keeping Gary and Mary's dream alive and infusing others with their knowledge and passion.

Melissa Poepping

Although I had been learning at your feet for years, the day you widened the circle to include me had a profound effect on my life. That day you embodied all that I had been learning from your coaching and the effect was life changing. Thank you for teaching me that I will be okay when the "garden weeds itself." You have opened my eyes to a new way of thinking and shown me how to be strong enough to set the boundaries for how I am willing to be treated and to carefully curate the life that I desire. Now that I am aware, I can no longer be unaware.

Thank you for teaching me to see it how I want to see it, with faith. Thank you for affirming my belief that there is room at the abundant table for all who come to give. You have demonstrated through your actions how to walk difficult circumstances while at the same time have a good hair day, keep your makeup intact, and own the stage. Thank you for not being a miser's chest and for selflessly sharing what you know. You are changing lives, and I am so happy and grateful now that I am one of those lives forever changed. This book would not have happened without you.

James and Stacy McDonald

It was Divine Providence that I found myself in your organization. God knew exactly what I would need. I had been fan-girling Stacy for a while before I saw her vendor booth across a crowded room. I decided right then that I was buying whatever she was selling. To any of you who question whether it's "worth it" to do vendor booths, Lori Borre enrolled at a vendor booth. (Just sayin')

Thank you, James and Stacy, for your wisdom, guidance, and leadership. You have always been there for me when I needed you and believed in me more than I believed in myself. You guys have been my biggest cheerleaders. You can't always look into the future to see who will be important and how close you will become. Stacy, I couldn't have predicted or known how much I would come to cherish our friendship. You guys are so much more than an upline. I have unending gratitude to God for putting that "yes" in my heart before you even asked me if I would like to try some oils.

Crystal Sewell

Thank you for showing me how to see things the way they really are and what true friendship looks like: fierce, humble and self-sacrificing. Strong friendship doesn't always need daily interaction, and no matter how far the distance, you have been there for me ***every single time***. You speak truth and empowerment and kick my butt as only you can do.

You have stuck by me at great personal risk, and I will never forget you for walking out on that ledge for me. You have blessed me in more ways than I can write in these few words, but I want you to know that I *love* you, I appreciate you, and I appreciate what you have done and who you are. You are the embodiment of integrity, and I am so humbled that you loved me enough. I hope I can repay even a small portion of the debt I owe you. I count your friendship as one of my dearest blessings.

Mindy Mandel

The day you called me and asked if you could sort me was the beginning of a beautiful relationship. You answer every question without shaming me and making me think I should have known the answer. You find things that I have lost without trying to teach me the file folder structure. You have these wonderful skills that I don't have, but you use them for the betterment of others and give them freely. You are the kind of person that makes an organization unstoppable. You are such a cheerleader for not just your downline but crossline as well as me. You are genuinely happy when others succeed. You are the true definition of a friend. I can't wait for the day when you finally release the power within you and you walk the stage. When that happens, I will be there at the end of the stage, losing my voice, taking the photos, bawling my eyes out, ready to give you the accolades you deserve.

Thank you for tirelessly working with me on not just this book but anything that I throw at you. You polish my thoughts and ideas. Without you this book would have not happened (or it would have taken a few more years). If this book is my baby, you are certainly the midwife. To my family, you and your family are so much more than friends.

Team OilyTown

Thank you for choosing to travel this journey with me. I see you. I see your tireless work, dedication, belief and heart. I see you stepping out of the paradigms that held you back, walking into the version of you that you never would have believed existed. You honor me, and you inspire me to keep going when I just don't feel like it. This book is for you, with all my love and gratitude.

Where Did I See That Again?
(Contents)

Dedication

I think this is the hardest part, for there are so many people I could thank.

He worked by day
And toiled by night.
He gave up play
And some delight.
Dry books he read,
New things to learn.
And forged ahead,
Success to earn.
He plodded on
With faith and pluck.
And when he won,
They called it luck.

For you, Daddy. This is for you.

Before We Get Started

If you want a pristine copy of this book, buy two. This manual you hold in your hand is meant to be used. The more you write in the margins, highlight the ideas that inspire you, star the sections that resonate with you, underline the techniques you intend to employ, rewrite the conversations in your own words, circle the ones that worked, and make your own sticky note tabs, the more this book will serve you. The more beat up the book, likely the faster you will learn. If you are like most people (and me) you finish a transformative book or attend an earth-shattering lecture, and determine to completely change your life. Then you go home and do the same things you've always done. Old habits and paradigms die hard, they say. But not this time.

This time, you will decide that you are indeed a capable, graceful enroller. You will tell your negative voice to sit down and shut up. You will picture yourself comfortable in that role. You will write affirmations in support of your desire. You will perhaps gather a few friends who have also decided to take the path less traveled. You will practice with these friends. You will practice on your family. You will re-read sections of this book and practice on the post office lady until you embody confidence. You will take mental note of every interaction and conversation. Enclosed in these pages is the road-map to take control of your own destiny and do it your way. This just might be the first book of the rest of your life.

Bon Appétit

Lori

A Journey OF PERSONAL DEVELOPMENT

"What we fear doing most is usually what we most need to do."
~ Ralph Waldo Emerson

When I was a new Young Living® Silver, Marcella Vonn Harting invited me to lunch while on board what will forever be known in Young Living® circles as… "The Compliance Cruise" (cue the foreboding music). Regulatory agencies and my company were changing how we could talk about everything, seemingly taking away our voices and our stories, and I was getting texts from my team saying that everything was too hard and they "quit." On top of that, because I was too cheap to invest in myself, I didn't purchase the text package on the cruise, and there was sketchy Wi-Fi, usually only available at 2 am from certain locations around the ship, so while I could receive texts in batches, I couldn't text my members back to encourage them to stay in the game. It felt like everything was collapsing; I thought it was all over. On top of that, I had left my six children for the first time, and I was missing them horribly and feeling like a failure mom. My spirit was at the lowest level you can imagine, and I think Marcella wanted to cheer me up, and cheer me up, she did!

After listening to my fears and complaints, Marcella calmly inquired, "What's your special skill? Everyone has one.

What's yours?" I replied without hesitation, "I could sell you dirt from your own back yard, and you wouldn't even know I did it." "Then," she said, looking intently into my eyes, "teach that to your team."

That admonition began my quest to understand the techniques that I used intrinsically, without even having to think about them. It took me years to study my own methods, take note of the things I said, be aware of them, and quantify them. When I was in the spirit of it, I was unconsciously competent (I didn't know what I knew) at sales. I didn't even know why I was successful, and that was a problem because you can't teach what you don't understand. Because of my background in sales training, I knew sales theory, but for some reason, hadn't merged the understanding with my own behaviors.

When I first started in Young Living®, this conversation with my downline was fairly typical:

Team member: *"Hey! I think I want to do this biz!"*
Me: *"Great! Do it!"*
Team Member: *"But how?"*
Me: *"Enroll/Refer someone!"*
Team Member: *"But HOWWWW?"*

I just assumed everyone knew what to do. It really is as simple and uncomplicated as that. Enroll someone. It is the first of three steps that walk you to the top of the company. The steps are:

1. Refer people. (Also called "enrolling" people.)
2. Recurring Orders. Help them love the lifestyle so they join Loyalty Rewards for life.

3. Help them refer their people. Teach them how to teach others about these amazing products and what they can do.

But HOWWW???

Fast forward to the fall of 2018. I had the incredible honor of being asked by my dear friends and enrollers, James and Stacy McDonald to share a stage with THE Marcella Vonn Harting at their IMPACT conference. After my little speech on "How to Enroll Your Uber Driver" which included prospecting and closing techniques, she addressed the audience. Out of her mouth sprang words I never would have imagined. "You need to write a book, and I will endorse it."

Well, when MVH tells you to do a thing, take it to the bank you had better do it. Mentors, after all, can see further than you can see. Another tip I learned from Marcella is there are two kinds of leaders who run into trouble – those who only do what they are told and those who won't do as they are told. Thus began the journey to do as I was told and write the book.

In the beginning of my Young Living® career, not only did I work on enrolling my friends and family, I worked vendor events. Goodness, I loved it. Talking to new people all the time about oily goodness? Yes, please! As I worked the tables and talked to the people, I noticed a peculiar pattern. People often said something to the effect of, "my neighbor's cousin's teacher's friend told me about oils once, but never followed up." People said this to me over . . . And over

And over

And over.

Someone had "shared" with them, but never closed. Never offered them the opportunity to change their life. Never told them about the starter bundle. Never explained how to unlock the 24% discount. Never followed up. Lost contact.

I began to see a PATTERN. Did people not understand? You can't say it once and figure everyone who wants to be a customer will chase you down for your referral link when they are ready to get started. Think about those ads that hound you on social media. Over and over like the waves upon the ocean, until you finally purchase. You have to keep at it, and you have to "close." Slapping some lavender on someone does not change her life. Helping her get started with the Young Living® lifestyle is what changes her life.

I started writing this book simply because Marcella told me to, but I quickly realized this was going to be important for my team. It would fill a need. Many times, no sooner would I get off an hour-long conversation with one brand partner (teaching them sales skills) than the phone would ring, and another one had the same question. Then another would call . . . and another . . . all with the same question.

The thought of writing a book for team YL, however, made me sick to my stomach. I still worried what others would think. I felt like I didn't have anything to offer, after all, there are others who enroll more than me. I am not the top enroller in the company. I am not at the top rank. I fail at so many things. I wasn't really excited about putting myself out there. ***Unworthiness issues much?***

Earl Nightingale cautioned that we all tend to underestimate our own abilities while at the same time believe that others are capable of so much more. That terrorizing feeling that hits your stomach is actually the same feeling as being excited like you're on a roller coaster ride. It's all in how you see it. Melissa Poepping, one of my mentors, taught me that when that fear hits my stomach, I could say to myself,

"I am so excited!" rather than "I am terrified." So, I put on my big girl pants and published the book. Tuck that lil' tip in your hat for when you are doing hard things.

Soooo, in spite of my internal fears, I decided to share with Team YL. Why? I believe we at Young Living® are doing righteous, necessary work. I can't worry about me. We are getting Young Living® oils into every home in the world, and I can't do it alone. This isn't just the latest network marketing craze. This is about life. There is simply no company on earth like Young Living®.There are other good network marketing (Or as Marcella says, Network "Thriving") companies, but nobody has products like Young Living®. We are a product focused company, which is why so many of our customers are just that... customers. If I wanted to stop my organization from purchasing, I couldn't do it. If I called them all up and said, "Hey, yo . . . ya . . . I was just kiddin'. I don't really want you to buy anything this month," how many people do you think would stop purchasing? Zippo. Young Living® has such a high subscription rate because we have products that you truly cannot purchase anywhere else in the world. We have products that change people's lives. The stories people tell are incredible, nearly unbelievable, and yet common.

If you've been around Young Living® for more than a minute, you've heard the kinds of stories I'm talking about because they are whispered in hushed tones at parks, events, and around kitchen tables everywhere. These are the kinds of stories you want to shout to the world. If you have referred people to YL, the texts you receive on a daily basis with some testimony of one kind or another about how someone's life has been radically altered tell you that this work is urgently needed.

I'm grateful for the people who sell kitchen gadgets, baskets, bags, trinkets, water treatment, towels, bras, paintings, balsamic vinegar, and pantyhose via network marketing. I often purchase from these companies, but . . . and correct me if I'm wrong . . . but, I've never seen a kitchen gadget, basket, or pantyhose create the kind of life-changing, generation-changing effect that the average person experiences with Young Living®. We sell tools with the potential to empower moms and dads, to give grandparents the energy to play with their grandbabies, to make happier kids, better teachers, better students. Our products make people more productive, heal emotions, build marriages, help people take charge of their own emotional and physical wellness, and help people step into their best life.

There has been a shift in the world. Have you noticed? People are beginning to wake up to the desire for natural wellness, clean eating and clean living. People are seeking out the forgotten remedies of the past that came without negative side effects or black label warnings, remedies that respect how our bodies are created to function and that work with our bodies rather than against them. People are realizing that the 84,000 (not a made-up number) chemicals that we have been unwittingly exposing our families to are in everything from our personal care and cleaning products to our clothing and furniture and are linked to the rise of all manner of dis-ease. People are searching out truly "clean" products, not just greenwashed clean products. We are at the center of the proverbial perfect storm of opportunity and if you don't mind me saying so, obligation.

Gary and Mary Young dedicated their lives to equipping every home in the world with Young Living® essential oils, and people want what we have. Most of all, they want hope.

Yes, indeed, the fields are RIPE for the harvest! But there are too many lives to be changed, and there is far too much on the line to think of competition. Competition is not a thing. I cannot do it alone. My team cannot do it alone. We must all do it together. Therefore, if my humble efforts can get us closer to the vision of Gary and Mary Young, then I'm all in.

This book is not designed as an exhaustive answer to all sales questions. Nor am I the only one in Young Living® who knows how to sell, obviously. Nor am I the best. But maybe, just maybe, my way will work for you. When I'm tempted to question whether I've really got this right or not, there's one thing they can't say. They can't say it didn't work. I believe I stand on the shoulders of the early pioneers in this company who were selling oils before it was "cool" to do so,

One
Person
At
A
Time.

Although this book is written by a woman who built mostly in person, I've been in sales long enough to tell you that people are still just people, and conversations are still just conversations. I believe these techniques are completely applicable to online friends as well. I have spoken with some of these social media rock stars who built their businesses very quickly, and they confirm my beliefs.

In fact, I consider myself a lifelong learner. I am enrolled at this moment in courses created by other YL Diamonds, Crown Diamonds, and Royal Crown Diamonds on mindset concepts and how to work the YL biz. Teachability is a hallmark of success, and that's why I show up regularly to put myself in the seat of the learner. Alvin Toffler taught, "The illiterate of the 21st century will not be those who cannot read and write, but those who cannot learn, unlearn, and relearn." And while I am firmly in the camp that we learn from everyone, if you want to be successful, you hang around successful people. Jim Rohn said that you are the sum total of the five people you associate with. Think about that the next time the price tag of a coaching program or a book scares you. I will pay to be in these other Diamonds' coaching programs until I can finish their sentences.

You don't just hear something once and "learn it." You must hear it over and over again because you are breaking old paradigms and repetition creates awareness. Awareness? What does that mean? We all take action based upon what we really believe and how we really feel. It is my job to change how you look at sales, or to increase your awareness, rather than just hand you a bunch of techniques to manipulate people. Manipulation is getting people to do what you want them to do, for your benefit. True sales, as you will see in this book, is the process of uncovering the needs of others and filling those needs for the benefit of everyone involved. So when you hear me say, "sales skills," recognize that I really mean awareness of how to serve others. As Bob Proctor says, "It's all an awareness."

Speaking of teachability, I have always been an insatiable learner and a voracious collector of knowledge. Much of what you see in these pages are ideas I have collected over the past 40 years. Truly, there is nothing new under the sun. I do so much collecting that I don't often recall where I heard it all. So, if you're thinking to yourself, "I've heard that idea before somewhere," likely you are right. When I remember where I first gathered or memorized a thought, I will name the originator and let you do a search for the rest of the story. But in some cases, I don't have any earthly idea how I first came to understand a concept. It is the hazard of being fully matriculated into the school of life, and I highly recommend this habit to you too because success leaves clues. **Find them.**

I also want to emphasize that I am not saying my way is the only way. Clearly, there are many people who have done this faster and with many different methods than mine. There are people who:

Work vendor events *(I do)*
Stay mostly man to man *(I do)*
Focus more on "attraction marketing" *(I dip my toe there but am not an expert at all. This book is NOT about attraction marketing.)*
Blog *(I don't)*
Teach classes *(I do)*
Don't teach classes
Have a hundred thousand followers on social media *(I don't)*

There are influencers: bloggers, YouTubers, and people who run Google ads. There are also people who don't even own a computer and built their business by riding their horse from farm to farm on the other side of the mountain. You see, there is no one way to do this. Well actually, there is . . . it's YOUR way.

This book simply represents my hat in the sales-conversation ring–my attempt to give you what I've got in the hopes it will bless you and your team with more tools for your toolbox, so that together, we can change the world. It is my attempt to be a center of distribution rather than a miser's chest (keeping what I know to myself for my own benefit). To God be the glory. Great things He hath done.

"May the words of my mouth and the meditation of my heart be pleasing in your sight, O Lord, my strength and my Redeemer." Psalm 19:14

Lunch with Marcella on the Global Leadership Cruise - 2015

Ron & Lori on the Global Leadership Cruise - 2015

THE ELEPHANT IN THE ROOM

"Give me a lever and a place to stand, and I'll move the world." ~ Archimedes

Young Living® Convention 2015: I was in the back of an UBER car. We had about 30 seconds left in the drive, and I went for it. I decided to close the driver and see where we got.

So I declared in my best preacher voice,
"***I believe*** our bodies are geniuses, designed by God to heal themselves if we give them the right stuff!
I believe we can replace all the chemical junk in our homes with safe, plant-based solutions that actually work, and cost less,
and . . .
I believe if the tree in the garden turns brown, you don't paint the leaves green and tack them back up! You do something to support the tree! And, if you believe what I believe, you belong on my team!"

The driver let go of the wheel, raised his hands like a praise and worship pastor, and proclaimed, ***"I believe!"***

And . . . that's how I enrolled my first Uber driver. There have been other Uber drivers too . . .

and random moms at the park
and soccer moms
and people at libraries.

There was the woman who backed into my car, the lady who sold me eyelashes, the front office gal at the eye doctor's, and the lady at the post office.

Anyone who has the ability to enroll with ease will tell you that, truly, we are surrounded by people who need Young Living®, but more on that later. I say these things not to impress you but to impress *upon* you what is possible because believing in possibilities is the first step to success. But I'm getting a little ahead of myself.

Let's take a timeout for a minute.

ALLOW ME TO INTRODUCE MYSELF

My name is Lori Borre, and I'm honored to represent Young Living® as a Diamond. But really, I am a homeschooling mom of six boys, living on an 80-acre hobby farm, in a dinky out-of-the-way town. Some would say my town was too small to support a business. I say that where you live is irrelevant. In fact, many things are irrelevant. Until recently, I didn't have a working website. No blog. I had no social media presence to speak of, though I did have a personal account on Facebook. My Instagram

Me After Enrolling My Uber Driver

account is new and has maybe 40 pictures. Yes, you can follow me, but do not despise the day of small beginnings. Many of my family and friends did NOT enroll with me. I wasn't famous or highly influential. I didn't even have a wealth of resources. Those naysayers had a point about what I didn't have going for me. In fact, it gets even deeper than that.

I grew up in a loving family with parents and brothers and a sister I adore. Sadly, my school life and church life were not OK. I was bullied from the time I can remember. I was also abused when I was four years old by an 18-year-old neighbor. These experiences led me, as a young teen, into other situations I won't go into, but they included spiritual abuse and isolation. Those experiences led me to life-long anxiety and panic attacks.

My weaknesses also made me vulnerable to predators, and I became a narcissist magnet, which created more trauma and chaos in my life. Somewhere along the way, I gained sixty pounds and my self-image tanked. It is only by the grace of God that I married an incredible man who was crazy about me and has helped me to heal from all these tragedies.

WHOA, Nellie . . . That's a load of vulnerability you just dropped there, Lori! I know, I know. I have a purpose. Those stories are a part of my past, but not my future. I only tell you these things for one reason. Sometimes, people look at those who are winning at life and assume their backgrounds must have been full of rainbows and lollipops, and that's why they are successful. They use it as an excuse as to why *they* cannot win.

I want you to know that if I can do it, so can you. Really, you can but, not if you're married to your excuses. We tend to coddle them and repeat our stories to anyone who will listen. I know because I used to fall into that trap too. But no more! Now I am a warrior who does not give in to those old temptations. Now, I realize that every adversity brings with it the seed of advantage, if only I would plant and tend it. Some would say that I had no foundation for building a business. People who say it can't be done should stop interrupting the people who are doing it. So, as I said, I didn't have a lot going for me, but I did have these three things:

> **Grit in my eye.** The kind that comes from being the object of bullying and disdain and from having to earn everything you got the hard way (by God's Grace).
>
> **A love for people.** The kind of love that comes from knowing that you never, ever, ever want anyone to be treated the way you were treated. The kind of love that only God grants—the kind of love that emanates from your soul.
>
> **Mad, crazy, sales abilities.** The kind that comes from repetition, grit, and a love for people.

MY STREET CRED

This book is about you, not me. Still, you picked up a sales book. Surely you care about the credibility of the author. I do love sales, and I think I'm somewhat qualified to teach on the topic.

I came by it honestly. My father was a consummate salesman who could sell a red Popsicle to a man in a white suit, and I grew up at his feet. I'll tell you more later about what made Daddy so good, but just know that I grew up believing selling was normal.

I cut my sales teeth on lemonade stands at the local swimming club when I was maybe six years old. I also flipped candy at school. I went door-to-door selling Girl Scout cookies and marching band cheese-and-sausage. I grew a large paper route, biked through the neighborhood raising money for "Jerry's kids," and, as an adult, hocked homemade fermented foods at local farmer's markets.

I even did outbound telemarketing *(Ewww)*. "Smile and Dial, Baby!" In fact, I made more sales as a telemarketer than the entire rest of the sweatshop room combined. I was regularly offered jobs by the people I called. My boss thought I hung the moon. I just couldn't understand why others weren't successful. All you had to do was *talk* to people!

Man, I *loved* door to door sales. It was a RUSH when the housewife started ticking the boxes and ended up with two of every kind of cookie! "Oooh, yessss, Lady! Yes! More Do-Si-Dos®! More Thin Mints®! You know, Lady, you can freeze those Golden Trefoils®!"

Other parents sold their kids' cookie or cheese and sausage at "the office" and won their kids' awards, but not me: Door-to-door, on my bicycle, knocking and talking, toe to toe. *#Winning*

When I grew up, I traveled across the US and internationally for about 100 nights a year as a sales and customer service trainer and consultant for companies large and small. Some clients you may recognize include Ford, Saab, Ocean Spray, Pontiac, Qualcom, Compaq, PartyLite, Helene Curtis, McDonald's, Roche Diagnostics, Nissan, RCA/Thomson Consumer Electronics, and many, many others. As a young, fresh-out-of-college newbie, I was schooled by Mary Beth

Ingram, a veritable genius of a woman, on all things service and sales.

What about Young Living®? In my first six years of active enrolling, I earned five of the "contest" trips that Young Living® created, so that means three trips to Hawaii and two cruises.

Royal Crown Diamond, Melissa Poepping once said, ***"Those who can, do. Those who can't, teach. If you find someone who can do both, listen up."***

BUT IS IT REALLY SALES THOUGH?

This question is the elephant in the room. I've heard it over and over again. I've even heard it proclaimed by people for which I have an abundance of respect. "You don't have to *sell*. You just have to *share*."

Listen, I appreciate why people teach it that way, and I think I know what they mean. They want to demystify the process and help people learn to tell their stories *naturally*. They want to make it safe for new people to help their friends and relatives. They want to lower the barrier to entry. They want to make the point that you don't have to be icky and pushy. They also recognize that sales gets a bad rap due to all the clumsy, half-baked, self-centered, me-first, copy-paste (ouch) salesmen out there, but, they may be buying into and perpetuating a false narrative: True sales is never being "that person." True sales is service.

Just as there are a few network marketing companies out there that ruined it for the rest of us because of their unscrupulous techniques, we've all experienced "that" salesman that made us cringe and caused us to run for the hills. *Nobody* wants to be *that* person! So, people hear that "shaaaare, don't seeellll" advice, and they take it too far.

With the best of intentions, they share
share
share
share
share
share
share . . . and get
nowhere but "broke island" because they lack the awareness or the will to close the deal.

In fact, I believe many people *are* sharing. On any given Sunday, if someone at church rubs their head, no fewer than fifteen women reach into their purses and whip out their Peppermint and commence the anointing.

People share with their friend, only to have their friend enroll with someone else, perhaps at a class where the hostess closed the sale, or with a blogger,
or with someone they barely knew on social media,
or with someone else from church,
or at a vendor event,
or at their doctor's office.

Not that there's anything wrong with enrolling at any of those places, obviously. It's just that if they are in, you want them in with you so you know they will be cared for!

Now, just because I insist that we are all in sales doesn't mean I don't love "sharing" oils! I love sharing! In fact, I don't understand why everyone isn't sharing. Seriously, when your neighbor comes over and smells your amazing house, she is going to want to get oils of her own! Help her get an account. Everyone should be sharing, even customers who aren't brand partners should be sharing. But I digress.

The unaware "sharer" is set up to fail because she doesn't have the whole story. She "shares" oils with someone a few times, but her friend doesn't buy anything. Then a few months later when her friend unwittingly uses someone else's referral link, the casual "sharer" simply doesn't understand why. She marvels at those who can "get people to buy a starter bundle," and she tells herself this whole thing may be for others, but obviously "isn't for" her.

Well, that situation . . . is a situation. Can we have an intervention?

If this, dear sharer, is you, keep in mind that your friend probably didn't even think you "did" Young Living® . . . because you didn't *close* them! Twenty years ago, people only knew one person who "did oils." Now, it seems, everyone knows several people who "do oils," as we notice with the church ladies. Who will they get started with? They will start with the person who builds trust and credibility and who *closes* them.

Why is this book called *The Harvest*? I want you to think about the farmer and how he operates. Does he spread his seeds around and then fail to go back and tend them? Does he stomp on the new little seedlings and tell them they aren't big enough for his liking? Does he demand the seeds grow his way? Does he abandon his field? Does he forget to harvest? Nope. HE GETS HIS BUTT ON A COMBINE AND BRINGS IN THE CROP!

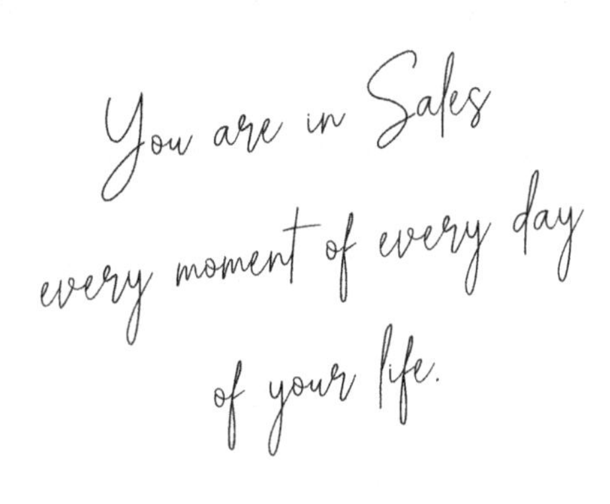

Spreading seeds is sharing, and it's good! I'm not hating on sowing seeds. But, if you are spreading seeds around, and you actually do want the harvest, then close the deal. You *cannot* be upset with the person who closed "your person." If **you abandoned your field, why are you upset with the person who harvested your corn? You obviously didn't want it . . . *or did you?***

No more whining that someone else signed up "your person." *We don't actually own people, do we?* Nevertheless, I want that to never happen to you again. People go to the person they believe is the best fit for them, and I want that to be you. I want you to learn how to harvest the crop you planted.

"But *really*? Sales?? *Really*??? I don't *WANNA* be in sales!" (Insert weeping and gnashing of teeth). ***Yes, sales!*** Do you expect the green beans you planted to hop into your basket without picking them? Would the farmer make money if he didn't gather the corn?

Let me pause for just a moment for you to get past the cognitive dissonance, then try one more time.

Yes, Virginia, you are in sales, but not just with Young Living®.

The dirty little secret is

Even if you never "do Young Living®,"

Even if you never generate an income,

Even if you do not believe me,

you are in sales, every moment of every day of your life.

You are constantly selling your ideas, beliefs, opinions, credibility, and, at the end of the day, your*self* to everyone you meet, from birth. As a baby, you cried to sell the idea that someone should come pick you up. In kindergarten, you sold "be my buddy."

Don't believe me yet? Let's take a look at some real life examples.
If you have ever tried to talk your friend into working on his marriage, *you are in sales.*
If you have ever tried to entice your husband or wife to take a vacation, *you are in sales.*
If you have ever tried to get friends to try sushi, *you are in sales.* If you have ever tried to talk down the price of a used car, *you are in sales.*
If you have ever tried to persuade your friend to workout with you, *you are in sales.*
If you have ever invited your friends to have dinner at the new restaurant in town, *you are in sales.*
If you have ever tried to influence your adult children to research a topic, *you are in sales.*

If you have ever asked for a raise, *you are in sales.*
If you have ever attempted to reason with your elderly mother as to why she should take her enzymes, *you are in sales.*
And if you have ever tried to bargain with a kid to do the dishes when it wasn't "his day," *you are definitely in sales!*
What am I selling in this book? I am selling you on the Harvest.

Can you see why improving your knowledge of sales and people will advance your success and your life? From parenting to business, developing an expertise in sales will help.

SALES IS LEARNABLE

The good news is that sales is learnable – *if* you are willing to change your mindset. All it takes is intention and practice. Now think about this. What are you good at? Did you pop out of the womb good at it, or did it require repetition? Oh, sure, there are natural inclinations, but every gift must be refined. Does anyone expect an Olympian to earn the gold without training and a good coach? Of course not.

While in Hawaii for one of the Young Living® contest trips, I had the pleasure of getting to know Brian Clay, Olympic Gold Medalist in the Decathlon, AKA World's Greatest Athlete. I asked him how he trained for the Olympics. I have never heard such a regimen in my life. Every moment of every day was focused and planned *for years,* in order to reach his greatest potential.

Every master was once a disaster. Our problem is we begin to compare ourselves to the "rock stars," and we take the "woe is me" trail. Even I have fallen into that, but it isn't a fair comparison. It's super easy to compare myself to people who have spent the past ten years building a following outside of YL and then join and become Diamond in what seems like a month. Their success appears to be overnight, but I promise you, it wasn't. You didn't see all the behind-the-scenes blood, sweat, and tears, the investment in personal growth, the elbow grease, the sacrifices. **The point is you cannot compare your beginning to someone else's middle or end.**

May I tell you a story? Once upon a time, I hired a team of elite brick masons, whose father had been a brick mason, to build a Russian stove in my home. For two weeks, these men labored in love over my precious brick masterpiece. Have you ever watched artists at work? They made a difficult task appear effortless, wielding their tools with the speed, superior skill, and manual dexterity born from years of diligence mixed with a dose of good genes.

Towards the end, they suggested I put in one brick, just to say I did. I eagerly accepted, certain it couldn't be *that* hard. Well, you can guess how that went. After 20 minutes of trying to get it right, they fixed it for me and pretended I had done it myself.

Because I stopped there, I am forever convinced that I would have made a lousy brick mason. What made me think I could have success the first time I tried? They made it look easy; that's what. If I had actually wanted to learn the skill, I would have had to dig in and practice, try, fail, learn, practice, and try again.

Are children born walking, or does it take falling down a few times before they get it right? My children have often heard me encourage them by saying, "Everything is hard until it's easy." So, is someone making Young Living® look easy? Be inspired by that, not defeated!

Not only does sales require practice, it requires time to master. When you are learning something new, awkwardness is to be expected. It feels funny, and too many people give up. Stick with it, and you'll be a sales MacGyver in no time!

Five years ago, I was not the salesman I am now, and I'm not as good now as I'll be five years from now. I can look back and remember many of the people I didn't enroll because my focus or awareness at the time wasn't at the level that person needed in order for them to be comfortable enough to jump in. I think "AAAAGH. If only I had thought to ask THIS!" But the truth is, we mustn't be judgy towards ourselves. It worked out exactly as it was designed to work out.

Give yourself the space and grace to learn. Consistent effort over time always wins the day, and if you keep at it, you won't recognize yourself a year from now, two years from now, ten years from now. There is no finish line in this game. There is no end to this journey. We never "arrive."

Every good salesman takes time every day to self-evaluate. What went well? What didn't? Accept the outcome and learn the lesson. Keep moving forward because the next person you talk to needs oils too.

One of the best ways to develop your competence is to sign yourself up for a vendor event somewhere:
The lady's church bizarre,
The craft show,
The Lion's Club Fish Fry,
The local farmer's market.

Unless you have already perfected prospecting and closing, do not go out and spend a lot of money on this. Please don't invest $1000 on the 40,000-person trade show. That's for later, when you are an enrolling machine! And, if you're too scared to do it alone, ask a member of your downline to go with you! It will be fun!

The goal is to get yourself in front of people. Spend $25-$50 max and file it under "personal development." If you enroll someone, that is a bonus. Your goal, your intention, is to hone your craft and learn to be immune to the "no." Hearing "no" over and over again helps you to conquer your fears. It shows you that the "no" isn't personal, and it teaches you to move on. The more people attending the event, the better.

You will quickly learn how to ask questions, present your product, close, and move on . . . in three minutes flat. You will soon stop taking it personally when someone doesn't want what you have to offer. As Mary Young says, "If this horse doesn't want water, go get the next horse!" You know, you might just change some lives in the process.

If we are aware that improvement takes practice, then why do we give up so easily? I see it all the time – someone tries to close one person (or have *one* class or work *one* vendor table), and when it doesn't work out, they quit. They lie to themselves, whining, "Well, I guess this isn't for me" (womp, womp, womp). "I'm just not good at it." "God closed the door" (heavy sigh). "If God wanted me to succeed, He would have blessed my efforts. He would have brought me more people." "The problem is I don't have a good upline telling me what to do or a copy-paste system." (sniff sniff)

Friends, this quasi-pseudo-religious-victim-mentality-nonsense makes me C

R

A

Z

Y!!!

Can you see my eyeballs rolling around in my head right now like Rosemary's baby?

We give God too much blame and not enough credit. How about we stop blaming God and others for our own lack of effort and start stepping out in faith? Mmmkay? If you want an apple, you can't "name it and claim it" and then lay in the grass and hope one will roll into your mouth. If you want the apple, stand up, get under the tree, and start picking. (Sorry. I tried to rip the Band-Aid quickly so it wouldn't hurt as much.)

SALES – AN ART *AND* A SCIENCE

Sales is both an art *and* a science. Like all art forms, there are things the artist learns through experience that can neither be quantified nor taught. It's the "gut" feeling you get that tells you when to say or not say whatever you're going to say.

This art can only be acquired through time and practice and, frankly, a healthy gut whose microorganisms talk to the brain. But that, my friends, is another book for another time. No one can teach you the art. Like most truth, it cannot be told. It must be learned.

This is why I chuckle when people want the *one* magical technique that works 100% of the time. They want the "Three Easy Steps" to Epic Builder. It is in our human nature to want everything to be cookie cutter easy, isn't it? There's no such thing as perfection. No, you must give art time to develop, and it requires awareness. But science? I can teach you the science. With persistence, patience, and grit, you will "get" this sales thing.

Let's refer back to our Archimedes quote in the beginning of this chapter. I believe that every person on earth can be "sold" if you give me a lever long enough. What is that lever? Time and Skill Set.

Both you and your potential prospect need time. You need it to develop your art, and your prospect needs it to break free from the paradigms that are holding him back. People enroll on their timetable, not yours. You need:

> Time for them to experience their own "aha moments."
> Time for people to break through their own paradigms.
> Time for your intuition to develop.
> Time for the student to be ready.

When the student is ready, the teacher appears. That means, when the friend you've tried to share with for two years is finally ready to hear what you have to say, you had better still be in the game. Listen up, buttercup. **You don't always sell your prospects. Often, you simply *outlast* them.**

> **Once someone gets on my "list," there are only two ways off. They enroll (with me or someone else) or they die. So, you see, you really do outlast people.**

You outlast their paradigms. You outlast their excuses. You outlast their poverty mentality. You outlast their spending habits. You outlast their circumstances. You outlast their business. You outlast their current obsessions. You just outlast them. (Notice I did *not* say to wait until you think you have the knowledge to proceed. In fact, waiting will only cause you to pay the "stupid tax," which I'll address later.) The point is to have patience with the process because you cannot control time.

The Rule of Seven says that most people require seven "touches" or presentations before making the decision to buy. Ninety two percent of sales people give up before the seventh touch. The problem isn't that the people aren't listening; it is that you stopped talking. When my organization hit Diamond, I had someone who sat on the fence for nearly three years call me up and say, "OK. I'm in." Me: "Whaaaa?" Them: "Yep. I'm in."

The other piece of Archimedes' "lever" is skill set, and unlike time, *this* factor is completely within your control. Isn't that excellent news?

Let's apply some pseudoscience, shall we? After nearly fifty years in sales, I created a made-up statistic that is based upon the Law of Diffusion and Innovation, and I have a deep conviction that it would be proven accurate should any academic decide to study it. I believe that with sales the bell curve is at play.

Three standard deviations (about 16%) of people on one end of the bell curve are NOT, outside of the grace of God, ever going to become a customer with Young Living®. Referencing the "lever" above, they simply run out of time to undo their paradigms. I mean, they might switch in 900 years, or maybe not. These are the types of people who will eat donuts for breakfast, binge on diet soda, and welcome all sorts of unknown prescriptions. However, these are the same people who are scared of plant juice, and believe it needs to be investigated and proven effective with numerous double blind placebo studies before they would ever risk their "health" by applying them. They are married to their diagnosis and their bleach. They believe chemicals are the answer, but they're fearful of the "germs" in nature. This, friends, *this* is not your target market. The only thing you are "selling" to these people is the next level of awareness. Maybe ask them, "Have you ever watched the movie *Stink*?"

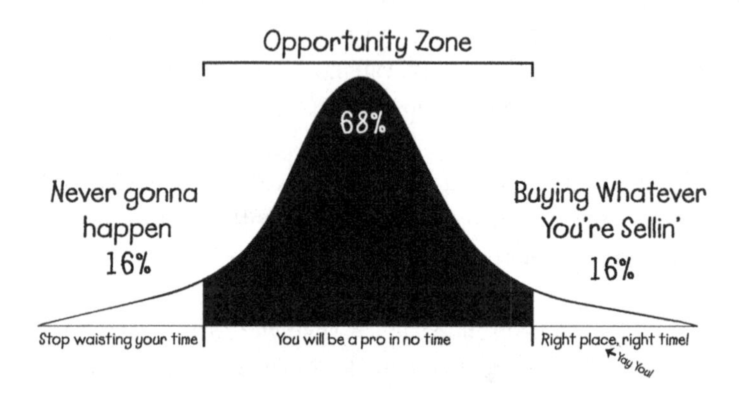

Three standard deviations (about 16%) of people on the other end of the bell curve are the ripe ones you're looking for—the low hanging fruit, ready to be picked! Stand under an apple tree at just the right moment, and you may catch an apple falling right into your hands. This is why you keep your "flip kit" with you.

These folks call *you* to get your referral link. They have been doing their research, looking into oils, and watching all the documentaries. They just didn't know you "did oils." But once they know, they'll buy anything you sell because they already love you. Closing these people requires little skill and is proof that **everyone** who wants to sell oils, can.

It is the two standard deviations in the middle (about 68%) where we learn who the salesmen are. So, do you see the opportunity that exists if you will simply up your game? Do you see how many more lives you could change if you just worked on you?

KEEP SHARING AND REFERRING

Step one to building your magnificent, natural oily empire is to bring in new customers. They may be your friend for life, and when the time is right, you'll show them how to turn their oily passion into a paycheck. Moreover, you want to continue to do this for the duration of your career. If you stop personally enrolling, your business stops.

In general, whatever rank you are when you stop personally introducing people to YL is the highest rank you will achieve. Obviously, you help others join your organization via their friends and family because as you have heard, "It's not who you know but also who *they* know." Helping friends enroll their friends is different than you bringing your own prospects to the table.

I'm talking about you personally bringing in new people. I'm talking about enrolling your ever-growing personal prospect list. It gives you credibility with your downline and keeps you sharp. It also maintains your relevance. Your downline brand partners don't care what happened ten years ago. They care what is working now.

Enrolling new people is also the **best** and **fastest** way to refresh the culture of your business. Young Living® Crown Diamond Kari Friedman taught me this:

> Don't like the negativity? Get some positive people!
> Not enough action? Grow some hot shots!
> Builders checking out? Find some new blood!

How empowering is that philosophy? Rather than complain about your biz, your downline, your upline, or your culture, just fix it. Enroll some new people! In other words, don't curse the dark, light a match!

What you do, replicates . . . just like parenting. Do you want your kids to eat healthy food? Eat healthy food in front of them. Want them to be nice? Be nice to them. Want them to go to bed early? You go to bed early. Want them to pray? Dance? Sing? Enjoy music? Use oils? Eat liver? You first!

Have you ever heard the advice, "Pull, don't push?" The concept is simple. Imagine your team all lined up holding a rope tug-o-war style. If you are at the front of the line, you can pull the rope and people will likely come with you. Some may drop off, but if they are holding on, they can't help but keep up. However, if you are at the back of the line pushing the rope, what happens? Nothing. People sit there holding the rope, doing nothing.

If you stop because it is too hard, you can bet your team will think it's too hard as well. In fact, if you stop for any reason, your team can feel it, and they will (likely) stop, too. They can smell it like a dog sniffs out fear. They figure it's time to lay off for a while because you did. Sitting around after you refer a few people, trying to convince everyone else in your organization to do their part (pushing), will get you nowhere. In fact, it's the number one mistake I see new Silver leaders make. They think they have reached a level where they can swerve into management mode. Oh, friends, don't do it. **Leaders pull; they don't push. Stay in SALES.**

Besides that, it's fun! Where are my ***BLUES*** on the color quiz?! FUUUUNNNN!!!! Of all the "sales" I have ever done, nothing has ever compared to the rush of a Young Living® "win." When you accomplish any achievement, you get a flood of dopamine, which increases your focus, concentration, alertness, critical thinking, and leadership. This is why "to do" lists are fun to check off, and why, if you do a thing that is not on the to do list, you add it to the to do list and then check it off. Go on ***GREENS***, admit it.

Another thing is happening in your brain when you empower someone to open a Young Living® account. They changed their life. You helped someone. When you help someone, your body releases dopamine, serotonin, and oxytocin. According to *Psychology Today*, dopamine, serotonin, and oxytocin hormones make up the "happiness trifecta" and boost your mood. Well, they also:

support learning, bonding, trust, and empathy,
improve your digestion and memory,
reduce inflammation,
lower social anxiety,
aid your sleep,
regulate your appetite,
aid wound healing,

and make you more motivated. But let's just stick with "happy." So, while selling can be fun, selling Young Living®, I believe, makes you a better functioning person.

I mean, is there anything better than getting a new member of the tribe??? It's just like having a new baby in the house! There is so much hope! Watching their eyes open wide the first time they "get it" or the first time a particular oil has the desired effect has got to be better than any other adrenaline rush. Then, you receive one of *those* texts!!! You know what I mean – the non-compliant ones, when someone had a non-compliant problem, and they used a non-compliant oil, and they got a non-compliant result? The feeling is nearly indescribable, and it keeps you going through the hard circumstances that may tempt you to quit.

On top of all that, referring (and closing) people is just the right thing to do. I've been told that Gary Young preached that "retirement" was a dirty word and that we were called to continue spreading the message until our oils were in every home in the world. Yes sir, Gary sir, I will always keep closing the deal because Young Living® is in my soul.

So, besides skill-set, which I *promise* we will get to, what is holding us back from growing our businesses?

MICRO-WORK and MACRO-WORK

There are two kinds of work you must do to build your biz. Micro-work and Macro-work. Macro-work is big picture stuff. If you're building your own courses, creating, designing a website, populating and babysitting a social media group, making pretty graphics, planning an event, researching themed notebooks, and crafting emails, you are doing macro-work. Want to know the biggest one that gets nearly everyone? Organizing your office.

Micro-work is the man-to-man, mano-a-mano, belly-to-belly, head-to-head, phone-to-phone, thumb-type-to-thumb-type, talking to the people work. Micro-work is relationship building and sales, and micro-work requires personal risk.

I see a lot of people make the mistake of macro-working like crazy, thinking they are busy building their business, not doing any micro-work, and wondering why their business isn't growing. I'm not saying macro-work isn't important. I'm not saying there isn't a time to do it. I'm not saying not to do it. Obviously, you will be more efficient when you organize your office. What I'm saying is you need micro-work, especially in the beginning, if you actually want your business to grow. So, why do people make this mistake? Macro-work is *safe*. It requires nothing from you. If someone doesn't like the picture you took, so what? If they don't like the color you chose for your office wall, who cares? Macro-work allows you to take a deep dive into busywork, and it fools you into thinking you are doing something. It masquerades as "building your business." It requires no relationship and no risk. Nobody is thinking you are "that" person when you are typing up your "oils and exercise" class.

Young Living® is a personal development curriculum cleverly disguised as an essential oils business.

Micro-work requires you to put yourself out there, to care about people, to empathize with them, to show a piece of you, and to take a chance. So, now do you see why people don't "micro-work?" They are *afraid* to do it.

If you're afraid of people or you're not successful when you are micro-working, you need personal development. The reality is that you won't go too far in this biz without personal development because what got you *here* won't get you *there*.

Well, step right up, because Young Living® is a personal development curriculum cleverly disguised as an essential oils business. Let's start with mindset.

MINDSET

Your thoughts affect everything. What you say and what you believe affect everything. Your mindset encompasses your beliefs about you, your abilities, and how the world around you operates. If you are "struggling" with bringing people in, I want to propose an idea to you. Is it possible that you are your own obstacle? Is it possible that because you *think* you can't, you can't? Remember Earl Nightingale? We tend to have a low opinion of ourselves while at the same time, for some strange reason, believe others are able to accomplish that which we cannot. Is it possible that you think being "an enroller" is not normal? You think it's only for the "unicorns?" The Others? The perfect? The
young enough,
old enough,
smart enough,
skinny enough,
pretty enough,
outgoing enough,
trained enough,
friendly enough,
healthy enough,
sick enough,
have enough time,
. . . and the list goes on. Excuses abound, and you know

what excuses are: lies you tell yourself that only you believe. We will tackle excuses later. For now, I just want you to be aware of all the "why I can't do this" thoughts that are flooding your mind.

When I started, I didn't have a smart phone or a laptop and didn't know how to text. But I did have one thing . . . grit. I had ***decided*** that by God's grace, I was going to sell oils to every person within three feet of me.

Sometimes, when I'm trying to help people see the opportunity that is all around them, they throw me the old, "Well, Lori. I can't be like you. I can't win the trips or sign up people at the post office." When people say that, I think (and sometimes say with my outside voice), "Come here in head-smacking distance and say that again." That makes me hot like a flame three feet high. What a cop out! People say things like that because they are afraid of the work it takes to learn to sell, so they try to put me on a pedestal to get themselves off the hook. (Ouch – another Band-aid® gone.)

Dig in and embrace the personal growth it takes to learn closing skills.

And who wants you to be me anyway? Don't be a bad version of me! Be an *awesome* version of ***you***! The truth is we are all the same. The only difference between you and me is that I have awareness around this topic because I've practiced for nearly my whole life. Listen, if a mom from a 900-person town in Indiana can reach Diamond, so can you. **If I can do this, anybody can do this.** Remember *that* the next time the comparison trap sneaks up on you and tries to convince you to *not* do this biz because you can't do it as well as "so and so." Don't put me or anyone else on a pedestal.

Instead, dig in and embrace the personal growth it takes to learn to close because if you don't close, they are going to show up at a vendor event with me or someone else and you'd better bet I will close them. Then, you're going to complain that Lori Borre enrolled your person and I'm going to say, "I'm sorry. I didn't know they were your person. I don't think they knew either."

Ooooouch. More Band-aids®! Are we still friends? (Covers eyes.) Aaaah! I hope so! I'm such a *yellow*.

Just so we're clear

Now at this point, I should probably pause to let the world know that I am a team player, and it is not my intention to harvest the fields others have planted. As a matter of fact, I have closed many people *for others not in my organization.*

I actually love the process of closing for others. When you've got no dog in the hunt, you can hard-close all day. You can really press the pain point. You can turn into *that* person and change lives right and left because nobody questions your motives. You can get bossy and pushy and take it to the mat. When I'm closing for someone else . . . I'm in the **zone.** *Lori rubs her hands and chuckles a dark, low, hehehehehe . . .* When I do this, my husband calls it "the full court press." I leave very little wiggle room.

> *"So, what's stopping you? No really. Susan has been telling you for two years you need oils, but you don't trust her enough to get in? Really? What's really going on? I know you can*

afford it because I just watched you drop $200 at that booth over there. Do you not believe they work? Have you not taken the time to look into the chemistry? Do you actually want to keep all those problems you just told me about?" – Hehehehe When you're closing for others, what have you got to lose???– *"I'll tell you what we're gonna do . . . Let's get Susan on the phone right now and we'll just get this done."*

One time at a health fair at a church, I closed six people: 5 for the church secretary and one for me. And oh, what a one that was. I tried to pass her off to the church secretary, but she wouldn't have it. She chose me. She and I had bonded, and we are still good friends. She is *my people*. And guess what? She has changed her *life*. I won't go into it all, but she made changes that will affect generations.

And the ones I closed for the secretary? I checked, and none of them got oils. None. Not one. Not with Susan and not with anyone else. Why? **Because Susan isn't closing!**

So, I no longer tell people to "go enroll with Susan." Rather, if someone tells me they want to enroll, but they feel like they need to enroll with "Susan, from church," I call their bluff.

Me: *"Awesome! Susan has been telling you about oils for 4 years, but you didn't believe her? Let's do this! Get Susan on the phone! We will grab her link RIGHT NOW and help you place an order! What is Susan's phone number?"*
Prospect: *"What?"*
Me: *"Yep! Let's get her on the phone now! We just need her number, and I'll help you get set up!"*

Now we find out if they were serious.

"HOW" IS NOT THE HARD PART

Why is the decision hard to make? *"What if I decide to do it and it doesn't work?"* Now let's think about this for a moment. Is everyone in the world reading your mind? Then who will know you decided? Nobody! You're the only one who knows. The risk here is very small. It just feels overwhelming.

I remember the day one of my upline called me up and asked me, "what do you actually *say* to people?" I didn't know how to answer. "I just talk to them" is all I had to offer.

I've read my fair share of sales books and too many are all theory and no practical advice on exactly what to say. I wanted this book to bridge the gap and be heavy on the practical side, so I will tell you *exactly* what I say.

Having said that, here's a little secret. The "how" of enrolling is actually *not* the hard part. The "how" is in this book and many, many others. The "how" is all over YouTube. The "how" is hiding inside you too. The **decision** is the hard part.

None of the **how** matters until you make the **decision**. You see, you don't learn all the sales techniques in order to convince yourself you can sell. That's not how it works. You *decide* to build a business, and *then* you learn whatever is necessary because you have demanded it of yourself. It is still true that whether you think you can or you think you can't, you are correct.

Consider parenting. Nobody knew how to be a parent when they had kids. You decided to become a parent and went from there. You read the books. You asked the people. You tried and failed and tried again. If I had to give one reason why our team made Diamond, outside of saying "the grace of God and an incredible team," I would say that it is because we decided we would achieve Diamond. Deep inside me was a knowing. **A knowing.** I had decided. Why? I knew I could change more lives that way. I knew I could do more for others as a Diamond. I could serve my team better and be more effective. I would have more influence.

Making the decision and altering your inner beliefs is the first step to accomplishing anything because what you believe, you act upon. Not what you *think* you believe. Not what you *say* you believe, but what you *believe* and emotionalize with. That is why I addressed what you believe about sales at the start of the book.

"Oh, but Lori," you say. "Feelings don't matter. Doing the right thing matters." Well, yes and no.

You teach your children to be nice even if they don't feel like it. You don't smack people in the face and call them stupid when you disagree with their opinions. You're not unfaithful to your spouse when you meet an attractive person. But in this case, I'm not talking about matters of "right" and "wrong." I'm speaking of the actions that you can take that will lead to success in any undertaking.

How you do the action is directly affected by what you believe and how you feel. Parents, you know this is true. Have you ever had a child wallop his sibling and then offer a half-hearted apology? How was it received? See? It isn't *what* was said. It was *how* it was said.

You see, I can feed you random techniques all day long, but unless you feel "in the zone," they will fall flat. You've got to be in the **spirit** of the thing. Not only will the tone of your voice and body language be affected by how you feel, so will your word choice. The energy you give out completely changes depending upon how you feel.

Think about the last time you were on top of the world. All the things were clicking. All the ideas were flowing. You couldn't say the wrong thing. It was incredible! How effective were you? Now imagine yourself making a call to a prospect when you are miserable and sad and can't stop thinking about your favorite pet who just died. What's the likelihood of enrolling that person?

TALKING TO YOURSELF

I believe mindset is the one thing that stops most of us, myself included, and mindset is affected by how we talk to ourselves. We fail to control our thinking, or worse yet, conspire against ourselves, which affects how we feel, which affects how we act, which gives us our current results. You will never outperform the thoughts you allow to float around in your head like so many unsupervised children. You will never outperform your own self-image. At the risk of repeating myself, I will repeat myself.

You will never outperform your own self-image.

Chances are good you say things to yourself that you would never say to anyone else. Would you talk that way to your worst enemy? Would you let someone talk that way to your children? I doubt it. Most of us would never be as cruel, hateful, judgmental or accusatory to anyone as we are to ourselves. And, here's a thought for you if you read the Bible. Who is the great accuser?

Mm hum . . . That was an aha moment, wasn't it? So, who do you think you are? Seriously, what gives you the right to talk to yourself like that?

You will never outperform your own self-image.

When negative thoughts occur to you, reject them out of hand. Do not say to yourself, "Well, that thought is true, and I need to be honest and realistic, so it can stay." If the thought makes you feel bad, sad, unworthy, less than, incompetent, or incapable, then reject it. (If it is something you have done wrong, then confess it, make it right with the person you hurt, and then forget it.) But talking like this . . .

"I can't do this like so and so."

"I'm not good at sales."

"I don't really enroll very many people."

"I don't know anyone."

"Enrolling is hard."

"I don't have extra time."

. . . does you NO good. Rather, speak *life* over this journey and yourself.

"I AM doing this."

"I have decided."

"The way will be shown. I am currently learning how to make this easy!"

"If others can do it, so can I."

"I love enrolling people and watching their lives change!"

"It feels AMAZING to talk to people and watch the light bulbs turn on."
"Every time I meet someone, I find a new friend!"
"I enjoy meeting new people!"

. . . and believe it with all your heart. That's the trick. You have to use the right words that paint a picture in your mind so you will believe the words you say. Find the piece of you that believes it and feed the feeling.

Mel Robbins talks about the Reticular Activating System, which is the filter through which you view the world. This filter only allows facts into your brain that align with what you believe about yourself and your world. Do you see why you must first change your filter? If you try these techniques with a negative filter about yourself, you will give up the first time someone says "no."

To change your filter, begin to speak kindly to yourself. No, I'm not kidding. Talk to yourself in that voice tone that a benevolent mother uses to encourage her young child.

"Well, look at you! You just met a new person!"
"See??? There you are! You're doing it!"
"Oh! You just redeemed those five minutes in the parking lot!"
"Why, look at you go! That person really likes you!"
"Oh! That was a new skill you just tried! Go you!"
"I see you listening for their need and really caring!"

The Bible speaks to the importance of staying in gratitude. "Be thankful in all circumstances, for this is the will of God for you." It also teaches us to control our thinking. "Whatever is good, whatever is right, whatever is lovely . . . think on these things." It also tells us to only speak Truth. "Take every thought captive and make it obedient to Christ."

Taking these concepts and putting them together is powerful. If you are a faithful person, pray the truth over yourself. Thank God in advance for what is happening, for the things you are learning, and for the community that He is creating. You deserve it because you are doing all the things required to deserve it. After all, you bought this book, didn't you? That purchase was an investment in you and your business, and an investment you make in yourself is the *one and only* investment you can never lose money on. It will never return void.

Our wallet and our use of time betray our true beliefs and intentions and just the act of reading this, mining for nuggets to make you more successful, even if it is just ONE extra tool in your toolbox, sends a signal to your brain that you are serious about your dreams and goals. Taking action on your goals is what gets you there. So, congratulations!

COMMON QUESTIONS AND SIMPLE SOLUTIONS

Prospecting and Closing

1. **Get around people.**
2. **Find the need. ("Pain" point. More on this later.)**
3. **Fill the need. (Address the pain point.)**
4. **Close the sale.**

For those of you who like lists, here it is, and it really is that simple. If you are not enrolling, it could be because you are missing one or more of these steps. Notice as we get into these techniques, they all fall into one of these categories. To be a consistent enroller you need to be aware of all four of these areas. As you evaluate yourself, think in terms of these four areas. If you are falling short, figure out which technique you are lacking in skill and work on that.

"OK! So, let's have the ACTION, Lori!
Let's have those TIPS AND TECHNIQUES, BABY!"

We're close. I promise, but if the tips and techniques are ornaments, you need a tree to hang them on, so stick with me for one more point. I will deliver the goods, I promise.

When people are "stuck" in their businesses, I repeatedly hear these complaints:

> *"I'm out of people, Lori. I don't know anybody else. I enrolled the four people I know. There's nobody else. It's time for my people to start enrolling, so I don't have to."*

Or its neighbor,

> *"Everyone I know is already into oils."*

Or its cousin,

> *"The market is saturated."*

HAHAHAHAHAHA . . . then why are others still having success? (Hear me clearly; friend groups get saturated; markets do not.)

(Get around people)

> *"I never know what to say to people."*

Or,

> *"How do you get people to talk to you?"*

(Find a Need)

> *"I don't want to be THAT person.*

Or,

"I don't want to chase off my friends."

(Fill the Need)

"I'm sharing constantly, but nobody is following my link!"

Or,

"I shared with so and so, but she went with someone else! I feel so defeated!"

Or,

"I just can't get people to get into the oils!"

(Close)

Prospecting and Closing go together like a horse and carriage. You'll see why!

Do you remember when I said I had three things going for me (grit, a love for people, and freaky good sales intuition)? You may be surprised to hear this, but of the three assets, it is the middle one that is the magic in the mojo.

If you try these techniques with the wrong motive, attitude, or branding, you will limit your own success. I know this from the bottom of my soul. It's the law of Sowing and Reaping.

If you are chasing only what you can get . . . if you elevate yourself above others . . . if you care more about the almighty dollar than you do about ***people*** . . . then people will see who you are, and they will run. Even if you fool them into a sale, they will eventually see right through you. People can *SNIFF* it out. We call this being "salsey." Are you authentic or not? Caring or not? This business is all about people. How do I know this???

Let me ask you a question:
Are 100% of your customers people or are they people? Am I right or am I right? Yes or yes? Knowledge of people will change your life in every area of your life. Oh, you might get lucky without understanding what makes people tick, but it goes back to that bell curve. How much *more* successful could you be with people skills? Who controls the money? The people. You work with people.

Live with people.

Eat with people.

Hang out with people.

Buy from people.

Sell to people.

Rely on people.

. . . and occasionally, need help from people.

Let's think about this; *my* organization knows you catch more bees with honey than with vinegar, and they are sweetness and light to all YL customer service reps, no matter what (said in my best Godfather voice). Do you recall that I was an international trainer and consultant who worked with call centers? I promise you this: Customer Service people *remember* stuff. They make notes, and they talk to each other, and they make subtle decisions about what to do or not do because they are . . . *people.*

So, if you want to get the best customer service,
go to school on people.
If you want to learn to prospect or increase your closing rate,
go to school on people.
If you want to earn more money,
go to school on people.

I want you to do me a favor. Think for just a moment about the best sales experience you've ever had. What three words would you use to describe it? Write them down please. As in, actually write them down. (No, really, go get a pen. I will wait.)

____

____

____

Now think about the WORST sales experience you've ever had. What three words would you use to describe it? Write them down.

____

____

____

Now then, as you look at those words, would they describe people or systems? As a sales and service consultant for over ten years, I asked thousands of people these two questions. The answers were predictable. In the case of an excellent sales experience, most people chose a mixture of people *and* systems. They answered with words like "fast, friendly, cared, listened, efficient, on-time." But in the case of a poor sales experience, the words nearly always came down to a description of the *people*: "Rude, dumb, pushy, talked too much, wouldn't take 'no' for an answer, fast-talking, and only cares about the sale."

The other common remark was that they would forgive the "system" issues if the "people" were on top of their game, but nobody was willing to forgive the "people" problems. Most people recognize that systems issues happen. Glitches happen. People make mistakes. Shipping delays happen. All is forgiven as long as they could tell that the person was doing his or her dead level best to be of service. But if someone was "rude," there was no forgiveness.

When it comes to sales, parenting, and life, your goal is to be "winsome." It is to communicate with people in such a way that people like you. Of course, this only works if you like them first.

If you try these techniques without a genuine desire to serve people, you risk being rightly perceived as insincere, stiff, pushy, or even like you are interrogating someone.

People don't buy oils,
they buy YOU!

So NO, you don't grab random people, wrestle them down to the ground, put them in a half nelson, and try to get them to join your Oily MLM Mafia. Nobody wants to be a rung in your Oily Ladder.

But . . . People DO want to join a movement. They DO want to be a part of something bigger than themselves. They DO want community. They DO want to solve their problems, and they ARE constantly asking themselves, "What's in it for me?" (WIIFM) and "Will this WORK for me?"

The first time I ever heard Marcella (nearly all of YL is on a first name basis with this woman . . . kind of like Cher, so let's just go there) speak, she talked about this. She said, "This is a ***relationship*** business. It isn't even about the oils first. It's about the ***people*** first." I took that to heart. I believed it to my toes. People don't care what you know until they know you care.

We must continuously build ***authentic trust*** and ***credibility***. Do you want the truth? Can you handle the truth? People don't buy the oils. **They buy you.**

If people don't trust you, you might as well shut the business down. People are always watching you. Where do you go? What do you say? What do you do? How do you dress? How do you appear? How do you carry yourself? Are you confident? Are you a product of the product? Are you using your oils? Do you have your oils on your person at all times? Are you using the supplements? Is there antibacterial soap in your house, or have you switched everything out for the Thieves® products? What is your body language? As a general rule, do you prefer yourself, or do you prefer others? Are you always seeking to learn more and to do better?

Are you leaving "the impression of increase" (Search that) upon every person you meet? That simply means that people are better off and more blessed because they crossed your path and did business with you. Or do you have a "taking" mentality? Are you someone who is trying to do as little as possible and still get the sale, doing only that which "benefits you"? Any ulterior motives?

Simon Chan, Network Marketing trainer, teaches that people buy your **change**, your **commitment**, and your **consistency**. In other words, your courage for speaking up, your personal changes that they can witness firsthand, and your consistency in message. Do you have that to sell?

Side leadership note: While I do believe you have to wisely invest your time with the "runners," I also know I've stopped predicting who "will" and who "won't" in this biz. How many people have jumped in with promises of how fast and far they would run, only to jump out when anything got hard? Alternatively, how many Royal Crown Diamonds said they would ***never*** build a biz? How many of ***you*** said that? I sure did! Some of my hotshot **rock stars** are people who said they would NEVER, EVER, EVER ***"Do The Biz."***

So if you think you're going to predict who will and who won't, I have a prediction of my own. You will be wrong. Often, customers fall in love with the product and then "can't help themselves" and decide to become brand partners.

People buy your Change, your Commitment, and your Consistency.

My father was one of the greatest "people's people" I have ever known. I told you my daddy was a consummate salesman. Let me tell you a little more. Born into silence with deaf parents, he took seriously his father and mother's admonition to love and serve the deaf community and others. It was his mission.

Many times he left the house at 3:00 pm and returned home after midnight, having earned a whopping $4.00 commission. He didn't calculate his gas money and figure it wasn't worth it; he just served. He made it his practice to provide $2 worth of service for every dollar he earned.

He didn't worry what was best for himself. He considered *only* the needs of his clients, even if that meant a lower commission. He was a people genius. It wasn't poverty mentality; it was people mentality.

And it worked out.
Because it always works out.
Because it is the universal law.

Which law? The Law of Compensation. Bob Proctor, author and speaker on the topic of success, teaches frequently about this law. He notes that we are paid in direct proportion to three things: the need for what we do, our ability to do it, and the difficulty there will be in replacing us. My daddy was a hard man to replace. Maybe, just maybe, Bob knew about my daddy. My father was irreplaceable. He gave, and he gave, and he gave.

My Daddy And Me

This is why he was a lifetime member of the "Million Dollar Round Table," one of the prestigious "Top of the Table" winners, and one of the most successful salesmen in all of the history of his company. It's why random people called him up and said, "Earl. I've got a lot of money here, and I want you to tell me how to invest it." Everyone knew and loved my dad. He had a servant's heart, not an entitlement mentality. The amount of "free" help he gave away was likely equal to the amount of business others sold. People (especially in his beloved deaf community) called and showed up night and day, needing this or that, and Daddy, to the best of his ability, always helped.

Recently, I witnessed a man in Starbucks signing to his computer, which told me he was communicating with a deaf person. I approached him, knowing that my father was well known in "the community." The man, who instantly recognized my daddy's name, told me that my father had interpreted at his parents' wedding, **fifty** years ago, and that he (this man) had attended my father's funeral.

People still speak of my dad with tears in their eyes. "Earl the Pearl" they called him. It is not lost on me that my name rhymes too. I pray in some small way that I am following in his footsteps. Oh, Daddy, may I honor you and make you proud in all I do.

My father didn't fear people because he served them. He talked to anyone and everyone. He talked to random people in the stores, at the parks, and at restaurants. He was hi-LAR-ious and always had a joke or funny story at the ready. He delighted the waiters and waitresses at the restaurants, calling himself "2% Earl" then surprising them with big, whopping tips. I suppose it is from him that I learned that there was no such thing as a stranger.

My father was driven to serve people. Years later, I read a book by well-known Rabbi Daniel Lapin who teaches about earning money from a biblical perspective. He asserts that we should be *obsessed* with serving God's other creatures. And when we serve, we eventually collect what he terms "certificates of service." We, of course, call it "money." You see, it is the *service* that matters. As Bob Proctor says, "You weren't put here on this earth to earn enough money to pay your mortgage. You were put here to serve."

As you read how-to "success" and "sales" books, both old and new, from different authors, from Bob Proctor to Brian Tracy, you find a consistent theme: serve, give, distribute, be other-focused, sow, help, be generous — the money will follow. In Thomas Troward's well known book, The Hidden Power, the author states:

> *It is not money, but the love of money, that is the root of evil; and the spirit of opulence is precisely the attitude of mind which is furthest removed from the love of money for its own sake. It does not believe in money. What it does believe in is the* ***generous feeling*** *which is the intuitive recognition of the great law of circulation, which* ***does not*** *in any undertaking* ***make its first question, "How much am I going to get by it?"*** *(Emphasis mine)*

Zig Ziglar said if you help others get everything they want, you will eventually get everything you want. Let that sink in for a moment. ***Everything*** you want. But it is first about the service. Be obsessed with the service, and the money will find you. Success will come for *you*. It can be no other way. This is not poverty mentality. The money is welcome. It is enjoyed and appreciated and invested into greater good. It is deserved. It has been earned. But the service is the main thing, and as Melissa Poepping says, "You have to keep the main thing, the main thing."

Interesting side note: How do you tell if someone is in it for the service or the money? Simon Sinek says that people have a "tell." What do they talk about *first*? ***Do they talk people? Or do they talk money?*** (Did Troward not teach us the same thing?) Listen to their conversations:

Salesman A:

> *"You can change so many lives! It's incredible the people you can serve! You just show up, consistently finding needs and serving. People need what you've got! What a difference you'll make in the world! Oh, and it is worth the effort. You can make your own economy!*

VS

Salesman B:

> *"Holy cow, I am making so much money! I just doubled my income from my old company. Everyone around me is making gangsta cash. It's so much fun to pay off my debt. Oh, and people seem to like the product. I've never had any complaints."*

***Did you hear what they just said: their "other company?" This is a red flag that they hop from one company to the next, chasing the easy money – the Will-O'-The-Wisp.**

Which do you think is the intention of our beloved founders? I mean, I haven't asked, and I could be wrong, but my guess is he didn't spend his life sleeping on distillery floors and traipsing through the jungle, risking his health and foregoing his sleep among other countless sacrifices *for the money.* My guess is she didn't abandon her singing career to dig in the dirt with her cowboy ***for the money.*** My guess is they made these sacrifices . . . ***for all of us.***

Gary Young and Lori in Hawaii

Isn't this what Troward was telling us? In the words of my father, *"Take care of the people and the money will take care of itself."*

"I never made a product for a profit. Only for a purpose."
~D Gary Young.

"All that lovely money in the hands of good people does great things."
~ Mary Young

Young Living®'s motto is **Wellness, Purpose,** and **Abundance.** I believe it is usually, but not always, in that order. We only get abundance when we bring **Wellness** and **Purpose** to others.

When people come to me and declare they want to make a lot of money and ask me if YL is the way to do it, I have learned to be wary. The lust for money sometimes causes people to compromise their principles, and those who chase only the abundance piece tend to get easily distracted by the next shiny object. I have seen it happen countless times. Some other company with some seemingly snappier compensation plan happens along, and that money-driven person disappears.

Why? Because in the beginning of your YL journey, you put in much more time and effort than you are directly compensated for. It isn't until later in the journey that your efforts can pay off exponentially. And what a journey it is . . . the amount of work cannot be overstated. Only Purpose will give you the grit to stay the course. It is the knowledge that you are part of something bigger, a movement, serving others, that drives you on, day after day.

Those who are doing it solely for what they can *get* out of it don't last very long. It's too easy to compare their current earnings to the hourly rate at Amazon and jump ship.

To stay the course, you must find your purpose. Your ***"Why." Why*** did God put you on this earth? What were you designed to accomplish? Many books have been written that help people to find their ***"Why"*** so I won't belabor the point beyond saying that it is your ***"Why"*** that keeps you from succumbing to the difficulties that threaten to hold you back. It is the ***"Why"*** that gives you the determination to keep learning and growing and doing until you walk the stage one day as a Diamond. So if your ***"Why"*** is powerful, then what's holding you back?

FEAR

Let's talk about some fears that hold people back. Even with all that ***purpose***, people get afraid. Afraid of what? Afraid of what others think. In Christian circles, we call this "fear of man," and it's a snare.

If you knew of something (sold on Amazon) that would help a friend, would you hesitate to refer them? Of course not! Then why do you hesitate when you stand to earn a small referral fee? Is it because you are afraid people will think you are trying to make money off the backs of your friends and family?

Well, *are* you trying to make money off the backs of your friends and family? Or, are you simply trying to serve? You see, if your conscience is clean, then why do you think people are thinking that about you? Do you think that about others? Do you harshly judge other's motives, or do you assume the best? Then, why do you think others are judging you harshly? Is it because someone said something to you once? If so, whose motives are being betrayed? *That* person's motives.

We tend to project on to others the motives that we ourselves have, so if you're afraid of "making money off your friends and neighbors" then you might want to check your motivations. If the problem is that you've heard others repeat the accusations, realize that has nothing to do with you, and as so many motivational speakers have said over the years, "Other people's opinion of you is none of your business."

Giving in to this fear of what others think causes hesitation, and hesitation causes loss. How many people could have improved their lives but didn't because you were too afraid to open your mouth? Moreover, how many people ended up enrolled with someone else where they may not get the care and attention you would have provided?

Remember the "stupid tax" I mentioned earlier? Do you know what that is? That's when you finally get up the nerve to approach a friend about oils and they reply that they just enrolled with someone else. Aaaand it hurts. I know. I've done it, both with family and with friends.

I can't tell you how many people have waited . . . and waited . . . and waited . . . and when they *finally* got over themselves, all their "besties" were signed up with someone else. Then, the would-be enroller whines something like, "Well if I had *known* you were interested, I would have invited you sooner!" (Enter head smacking.) NOPE. That's not how it works. It's your job to get out of your comfort zone and *talk* to your friends, not wait until your friends are "interested in oils" and show up at your door.

Now having said that, God is sovereign. People end up on the teams they were designed to end up on. Move on and go enroll someone else. *But keep the lesson.* Always remember: you get to *keep* the lesson! The lesson is to **Do It Now**. I promise you this . . . if you hesitate, you will regret it, and if you give up, you will always ask yourself if you could have done it. Nobody wants to live with that kind of regret, and nobody wants to be on their death bed wondering what would have happened if they had just given it their all.

GETTING PAST YOURSELF

It is the love of people that will banish the fear of people. Oh, friend. Maybe you think I'm laying it on a little thick, but I don't think so. I believe we are under a *moral obligation* to serve our fellow man, to distribute our knowledge to those who will hear. **How do you sleep at night** if you don't share oils? Seriously, if you aren't telling others . . . **Why?** No really, **why?**

Let me ask you a question. Have you ever experienced a life changing result from a Young Living® product? What if nobody had ever told you? What if your baby had not started sleeping through the night? What if you were still in bondage to your local "corner store?" What if you hadn't kicked the chemicals out of your life? What if you didn't have tools at your fingertips to make you a better, more capable parent? What if your hormones were still a mess? What if you were still on all those meds? What if you hadn't saved so much money not running to the doctor constantly for every little thing? What if your kids were still sick all the time? What if you had never been able to have that baby "they" said you couldn't have? What if you hadn't ever learned what all the toxic chemicals were doing to your reproductive system?

Do you not see the people drowning in their chemical ocean? Do you not see the hurt? The heartache? The bondage? Do you want a better way for them, just like you want for yourself and your family? What is the golden rule? "Do unto others as you would have others do unto you." In other words, "What I want for myself, I want for everyone."

Friend, there are people right now *praying* for God to send them answers! They are up at 2:00 and 3:00 in the morning, hopeless and hurting, face on the ground, begging for someone who knows anything about how to live a better life to find them. Praying for *you* to find them.

> "Oh, Lord PLEASE! Everything feels so hopeless! My son isn't able to focus in school and the IEP meeting is coming and I don't know what to do but I'm so tired because I'm not sleeping well and I don't have any money because the water heater went out and I'm so sad I just want to cry all the time and I don't see any hope . . ."

Buuut, you're too afraid to tell your story? You don't want to be "that" person? What if the person was drowning in the middle of the ocean? Would you not toss them the life-preserver? ***Aaaagh, Lori pulls her hair out!***

YELLOWS, can I talk to you for a moment? Did you hear what I said? People are *praying* for you, but you won't share oils? Really? Don't be selfish. Don't be prideful. Your story matters to people, and they need to hear from you. You are the person that God can use to answer that 2AM prayer . . . if you decide to be. The point I am making, and perhaps it will help your thought process, is that sales is actually . . . service.

So, where do you find all these people? Isn't the market already saturated? (Lori chuckles) No! Friend groups can be saturated. Churches can be saturated. The *market* is never saturated. If I am still enrolling people, why can't you? Search how many people turn sixteen every day. Young Living® has told us that no state has more than 1% of the population as members. That isn't saturated. You are swimming in an ocean of opportunity. Opportunity is ***every***where for those who are ***aware*** enough to see it. How many people can you think of who need oils?

Let me help you out. There are four groups of people to talk to, whether on social media or in person:

Hot Market: "besties," close friends, and close relatives.

Warm Market: distant family, friends, and closer acquaintances.

(Everyone knows we want to enroll these two markets. Somehow, people tend to dismiss the other two markets.)

Lukewarm Market: Neighbors you know, acquaintances and people who may be able to pick you out of a lineup, but aren't friends. Also, friends of friends and old friends and acquaintances you haven't seen in a while.

Cold Market: Neighbors you don't know. These are people at the park, stores, vendor events, and random followers on social media. I hear you say, "but Lori, is it really practical to enroll people off the street?" Ummmm, yes, Yes, it is. I mean, I enrolled someone with whom I had a car accident. So yes, yes, it is practical.

Now, ask yourself. Which of the above four groups contains the largest number of people? Your mind just expanded, didn't it?

Every friend.
Every Uber driver.
Every sibling.
Every aunt or uncle.
Every co-worker.
Every checkout cashier.
Every person on Instagram.
Every hotel maid.
Every worker at Lowe's.
Every person in your contact list.
Every shopper at Lowe's.
Every worker at the post office.
Every worker at the Burger King.
Every person at a farmer's market.

Every person you went to high school with.
Every librarian.
Every cabinet maker.
Every accountant.
Every secretary.
Every doctor.
Every nurse.
Every veterinarian.
Every hair stylist.
Every nail technician.
Every teacher.
Every coach.
Every decorator.
Every plumber.
Every electrician.
Every waiter.
Every waitress.
Every neighbor on a walk.
Every committee member.
Every soccer mom.
Every baseball mom.
Every dance mom.
Every person at your place of worship.
Every mom at the park.
Every barista.
Every person in the parking lot at the Kroger.
Every home on the planet.
. . . needs Young Living® oils.

Now that you're in the right head-space . . .
Now that you're confident in your motives . . .
Now that you see the opportunity . . .
Now that you know you can . . .

Now that you've decided to . . .
Now that you are fearless . . .
Let's look at the process.

It is the love of people that will banish the fear of people.

Gary photo-bombing Lori on Santorini Island - 2015

Gary, Mary, and Lori on the Global Leadership Cruise 2015

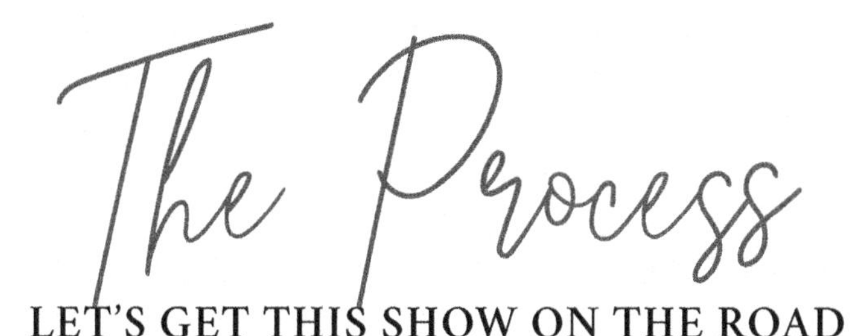

The Process

LET'S GET THIS SHOW ON THE ROAD

"Make new friends, but keep the old. One is silver and the other gold." ~ Girl Scout camp song based on a poem by Joseph Parry

Remember the four steps we talked about before? When you strip away all the advice and fluff and techniques and how-tos, the process of enrolling people really is pretty simple.

1) Get around people.
2) Find the need.
3) Fill the need.
4) Close the sale.
Keep these steps in mind as you read.

Expand Your Network

If this biz is all about the people, and it is, you've got to get around people, in real life or online. I look at network marketing as **Multi Level Friend Making**. He who expands his network the most . . . wins. So really, you and I are professional friend makers. I once heard Royal Crown Diamond Jordan Schrandt say, "It's just like being in kindergarten. You walk up and say, "Hi. I'm Jordan. Wanna be friends? Then you take it from there." Man, did I write that one down!

Or . . . did you think maybe the way to do network marketing was without networking? You can expand your network by getting out of your house, or you can do it on social media, but you must expand your network.

In person, people are everywhere. No really, **e v e r y w h e r e .** Prospecting everywhere you go is how you squeeze this biz into the cracks of time, as you go about your busy life.

Once, I made a new friend in the parking lot at the Kroger. She was heaping groceries into her car, and I said to myself, "I'll bet we have a lot in common. Nobody hoards food like that unless they have a ton of kids or are running a school cafeteria."

> **So, I remarked aloud,** *"Wow, not many people do groceries the way I do!"*
> ***She laughed and exclaimed,*** *"Well, I have 5 kids."*
> **Me:** *"HA, see? I have 6. Folks have no idea, do they?"*
> **Her:** *"No, Girl."*
> **Me:** *"Do you live around here? We should be friends."*

We follow each other on social. BAM. One more person on **DA LIST**. Did she enroll that day? Nope. But she might . . . One day, she might . . .

The other way to expand your network is on any of the jillion social media platforms. Some people think this is "the easy way." Others believe this is how you can refer people without actually needing to form relationships. Those people would be wrong.

I have extraordinary appreciation for those who build mostly online, and I would venture to say that they work every bit as hard as the "in person" builders, and they ***do*** have relationships. Those Instagram and Facebook rock stars will be the first to tell you that online people are still real people, and that in some ways, it can be harder to build those relationships online than in person.

Entire books have been written on the niche of how to grow your network online, but let me just mention one technique that I've used successfully on social media. It's called CLAM.

Joining groups based upon your actual hobbies and interests is a great way to "meet" new friends. When you're in these groups, you just interact. You be real, and you keep your eye out for people who think how you think and have similar interests. In other words, you look for "your people." When I see someone who is likeable, fun, a young crunchy mom who ferments veggies and quilts, is positive and cheerful, and leans towards my view of the world, I take note. If that person doesn't have a bunch of mutual friends with other Young Living® Brand Partners, I take special note. I look at their profile to see if it mentions YL. If that person makes a random post or asks a question I know the answer to, I employ the CLAM technique. I:

Comment (on the post)
Like (or "love" the post)
Add (that person as a friend) and
Message them.

Let's look at an example.
Original post:

> *I am frustrated with all the weeding in my garden. Does anyone have any ideas what to spray that isn't totally toxic? I've got 3 boys, and I don't want them around the nasty.*

My Comment:

Girl! Have you ever heard of "Back to Eden" gardening? Here's a link!

Like (or better yet, love) the post.

ADD as friend.

Private Message:

We've done "Back to Eden" for four seasons now. It isn't perfect, but it's a total game changer. Do you want to chat? I can totally walk you through it.

Notice I did not sell oils on the post or in the message. I served and built relationship. I built trust. I made a new friend, whether she ever gets oils with me or not.

Again, I cannot squeeze into a few pages what could take a book to explain, but let me give you one caution about social media. Do *NOT* cold message people, "Hey! You have such cute kids, and your page is so rad, you could totally do what I do and earn a bunch of money!" (Sends income disclosure statement.)

No No No No No No No No.

It may "work" for some people, but it attracts people who are desperate or money driven, and it feels icky and smarmy. Doing that is not authentic and real. Do not spam random people.

Someone once said to me that this "friend-making" thing was predatory. Well, that person actually didn't say it *to* me. She said it *about* me, which is usually how gossips work. My response? I shrugged and said, "Ummm... OK. Wow. I thought we were trying to get oils in the homes of everyone on the planet. I thought we were filling an incredible need.

And I thought you really liked people." Oh well, moving on. Shaking the dirt off my shoes.

If you don't like people and/or are in this thing for your self-interest, then that may be more applicable. But, if you are willing to just enjoy being friendly, whether or not that new person ever becomes a customer, then how could anyone be against that? Remember, you are *serving*. You already have your oils, and you use them like a ninja. You don't need that person. They need you. Fix this one idea firmly in your mind: they need you more than you need them. They *need* you. And ultimately, if you don't close them, someone else will.

OK but *how* does getting more followers on Instagram or friends on Facebook or friends in real life lead to customers? I'm glad you asked!

MAKE YOUR PHONE RING

One method to gaining a customer is to *attract* them. What does that mean? You are a product of the product. You genuinely share on your social media (and in person) what you are doing. Yes, Virginia, people actually do care what you are doing, just like that old movie, The Truman Show. They care what you're making for dinner . . . what you use on your face . . . how you help your littles sleep . . . what your bedtime routine looks like . . . how you're dealing with your stress . . . how you are working with your seasonal sensitivities . . . how you lost weight . . . why you look so young . . . why you are feeling so much better . . . what crafts your kids are making . . .what your home school looks like . . . what you're growing in your garden . . . the quilt you just made . . . what you use to wash your dishes . . . how you manage chores . . . what your decorated kitchen looks like . . . what oils you're using in your diffuser . . . what books you're reading with your kids.

Along the way, they will notice you just being you, which authentically includes Young Living®.

When you share on social media, all those new followers and "friends" are seeing your message. If you do it well (which is another book), people will actually reach out to you and ask you about your product. Do you think it's easier or harder to get a customer when that person calls you? Exactly. Having said that, there is an art in helping people come to the table. Ask questions.

YOU JUST TALK TOO MUCH

Let's remind ourselves what we talked about in the last chapter about your "worst" sales experience ever. Think of those words you wrote down. Pushy. Salesy. Didn't care. Rude. Talked too much. Now recall the best sales experience you've had. Likely the salesman behaved like a trusted advisor, asking you questions to glean exactly what you were looking for. Keep that person in mind as we go through this section.

People are somewhat predictable. They will tell you exactly what you need to know to close them, if only you will listen more and talk less. Most salesmen are clumsy and talky. Very, very talky. Let's take a look at why most of us talk too much. I think there are four reasons for this.

First, it feels good to talk about ourselves and our passions. Science tells us that when we talk about ourselves, we trigger the same pleasure sensations in our brain as money or food. According to a May 2012 article in the Wall Street Journal, researchers at Harvard University offered test subjects money if they chose to answer questions about other people rather than themselves. Despite the financial incentive, volunteers willingly gave up between 17%-25% of their potential earnings by choosing to talk about themselves. Well friends, we give up much more than that when we verbal vomit all over people.

It feels good to talk about our oils or our NingXia Red® because it is one of our favorite subjects, especially if we have had one of *those* experiences, which we all most certainly have had. So, brain crack + passion = what my father called "diarrhea of the mouth." The solution? Give someone else the fun of talking about themselves. You'll thank yourself.

Second, we are unprepared and/or tired. We don't know what question to ask, so we revert to what we know. We talk about us, the changes we've seen, the stories we've heard, the experiences we've had, the research we've done, and the people we've helped . . . the features, advantages, and benefits of Young Living® . . . the farms . . . the Sourcing, Science, and Standards . . . the Seed to Seal . . . Gary Young . . . the trips . . . the paychecks . . . the ranks . . . the awards . . . anything we can think of because we're just SO excited to "share" YL! This habit can also bite us in the back side when it comes to giving our "presentation" or "message" because when we're unprepared, we tend to ramble.

So, use your oils, get your sleep, and look up "pithy." When in doubt, say *less*, not more.

Next, there is self-importance. We know so *much*, especially if we've been doing research or have had life altering experiences or have helped others in remarkable ways, and we just want to take a needle and inject the goodness into all the people! It can come across sort of like being a professional show-off. We think everything we have to say is so important that we just keep talking. Ouch. I've done it. We've all done it. But, people are far less impressed with us than we are with ourselves.

We were given two ears and one mouth for a reason. If you will just shut up and listen, people will tell you the very words to use to close them. Keep in mind that this isn't about us; it's about *them*!

Maybe consider breaking out the Humility oil? After all, Gary Young taught us that you can't have Abundance without Humility. Last, we have anxiety. Have you ever been there? The silence was maddening, so you just started talking and didn't know when to stop? I have. *Ugh.* It's so painful, even when you're in the middle of it. It's like an out-of-body experience. You're in the upper corner of the room, watching yourself, thinking, "Shut up," but you just kept going. And the more you try to make it better, the worse it gets.

Ellen DeGeneres did some excellent shtick over the years by imitating this need to fill the silence by "over-talking." What makes it so funny is that it is so true. If this describes you, may I suggest some Valor®?

I'm not saying there is never a time to tell your story. Oh, there is, but, what if I told you that you could tailor your presentation and your "close" to the person you're talking to in such a way that hits so close to home that they can't help but say "yes"? That's where the ninja use of questions comes in.

Let me bring this home for you. Remember the four steps outlined above (Get Around the People, Find the Need, Fill the Need, Close the Sale)? Have you ever met a salesperson who skipped number 2? Have you ever been 1, 3, 4ed? Here is what this sounds like:

> *"Hi, my name is Lori; it's nice to meet you. My family used to be in and out of the doctor's office constantly like a revolving door, but last year my kids got the perfect attendance award. I have some oils on me. Do you want to buy a kit?"*

As a reader, how does that strike you? Icky? Salesy? An advertisement? Someone chasing the money?

Now that you know what that feels like, you'll never want to do that again. Learn the skills to get people talking, and you will never do that to anyone again.

Ron & Lori In Hawaii for Drive to Win Contest

2016

Lori helping plant trees at the Sandalwood Reforestation Project

How TO FIND AND FILL THE NEED

"I never learn anything talking. I only learn things when I ask questions." ~ Lou Holtz

THE IMPORTANCE OF QUESTIONS

Do you remember when we said that we are in the relationship business, that what we are really doing is Multi-Level-Friend-Making? Asking questions and being interested in others is being a good friend, and it also has other benefits.

Asking questions subconsciously puts you in the role of consultant rather than salesman, especially if you posture yourself in confidence with a knowing look on your face. You know the look – that expression that means, "I am *totally* into what *you* are saying, and I may or may not know more than I am willing to say." Making people beg for your opinion can be very effective. In fact, if it's a serious topic, I have learned to ask, "Do you *really* want to know?" I'll tell you this: when you ask first, it saves you a lot of time because you don't chase people and don't waste an hour explaining something they really didn't want to know.

Asking questions makes the prospect think about their *own* circumstances in a new way. It re-frames their thinking in the terms you want them to ponder.

Asking questions controls the conversation. **He who asks the questions is in control of the conversation.** Why do you think that in a court of law the witnesses are asked *questions*? The questions control the narrative. All you ***REDS*** just sat up straight, didn't you? Admit it.

Asking questions allows people to talk, and if people talk with your guidance, they often talk themselves right into the sale. Nobody likes to be "sold," oh, but friends . . . people *love* to buy.

Asking questions uncovers the need (that you will fill with Young Living®). It gets people to tell you everything about their hopes, dreams, goals, motivations, and pain levels. What? Pain? What does that mean?

Thirty years ago, I learned (from David Sandler's Sandler Selling System) that people buy to avoid or eliminate pain. What kind of pain? Emotional pain, physical pain, spiritual pain. All kinds of pain.
We buy coats
to avoid the pain of being cold.
Tweens and Teens buy the right kind of shoes
to avoid the pain of being singled out by a bully.
We buy washing machines
to avoid the pain of going to the laundromat.
We buy coffee
to avoid the pain of trying to get through the day exhausted.
We buy deodorant
to avoid the pain of not having any friends.

Some of us buy the latest car
to avoid the pain of not keeping up with the Jones's.

The dentist is the best salesman in the world. He or she has you convinced that if you don't go in to see him or her every six months, you are going to be in pain. There are many theories of sales, and as a professional trainer, I've seen 'em all. This is one of the truest ones I've ever encountered.

Think about it. In Young Living®, there are all kinds of pain to be found. Sometimes it's literal pain, as in discomfort. Looking deeper, it could also be the pain of not having other mom friends who "get it." The pain of not having community. The pain of no wiggle room in the budget. The pain of having no solutions to problems. The pain of dropping their kids off at daycare when they would rather stay home and be a momtrepreneur. The pain of not having quality products to use rather than toxic chemicals. The pain of debt and worry every time the car breaks down.

Questions help you locate the pain. And when you know the pain, you know where you can serve. When you know the need, you can help fill it. Now, you can truly help people create the perfect, customized beginning to their oily life, so what you're really saying to people is, "Hi! My name is _______. Tell me where it hurts."

One of the many things I love about my husband Ron is his ability to listen. He has always been the best question-asker I've ever known. Early in our marriage, a certain pattern emerged. We would go to dinner at someone's house, and he would come home knowing the host's entire life story including all the details. Meanwhile, I was on the couch talk-a-holic-ing from anxiety. I just couldn't figure how he did it. How did he know what to ask? So, one time on the way home, I asked him, "How do you know what question to ask?" "I'm just interested," he responded.

Huh. Pause... Hmmm... Thinking... Think, think, think...

So, the next time, I tried that. I was genuinely interested in people, but I still didn't know what to ask, so I sat there and stared at the person until the silence was deafening and then ... lost control and verbal vomited some more! It was ***awful.***

Eventually, I learned some techniques, and I'm going to teach them to you. Anyone can become an incredible listener if you will just learn these secrets.

Be aware; if you're in a warm market, asking these questions seems simple and natural. However, if you're in a cold market, it can feel awkward, so people freeze up. Before you randomly start asking questions of a stranger, you need an ice breaker – a reason to talk.

The best most incredible way to make others want to get to know you instantly is by saying something funny. You heard me right. It doesn't even matter the situation. This little tip can work in a job interview or a baseball game. Make eye contact and if they hold it, it's your cue to initiate a conversation, no matter how short.
(At a kid's softball game)
"Hi! I'm Lori. Are you with the right team or the wrong team?"
Ha!
Wait for the ref to make a bad call, and then break the ice.
"Is he with us or them?" Ha!
(At a swim meet)
"Is that your little rock star down there?" Ha!

"That kid is incredible. He's yours, right? I'm sure he gets it all from you." Ha!
(At a paint store or any retail outlet – to the worker)
"I was told you know everything." Ha!

Then you can ask questions. Sometimes it will feel right to do it then. Sometimes you will wait until next time. You know, just like real people do.

QUESTIONS MADE SIMPLE

There are a few acronyms I use to help keep me on track. The first one is **FORD**. You simply ask open ended questions about the other person's

Family
Occupation
Recreation
Dreams/Goals

But not necessarily in that order.

"So, tell me about your family!"
"What do you do when you're not running around at soccer fields?"
"Do you work a day job in addition to your mom gig?"
"Do you have family in the area?"
"Do you have any babies or fur babies?"
"When you aren't at your day job, what do you do for fun?"
"How many do you have?" (to moms at the park)
"Do you live around here?"
"What do you love about your occupation?"
"What got you into that?"
"What made you want to be a XYZ?"
"What do you love about it?"
"How did you two meet?"
"When did you know?"

The Dreams and Goals questions are usually an outflow of something they have said, like if they are wanting to move, or attend school, or have more children, or go on vacation, or change jobs or build a dream. You say, "Oooh! How exciting! When will you be able to do that?"

Sometimes, if you have enough relationship with the person, or suppose you're meeting a new friend for tea, you can get deep. "Tell me your story." "What does the future look like for you?" "What kinds of things are you doing to support your health?""What do you want most out of life?"

Here's a good one if you are seeing an old friend. "It has been *so* long since I've seen you. Catch me up. Start at the beginning and tell me everything, and don't leave anything out."

People don't care what you know until they know that you care.

The next memory trigger is FORM, very much like FORD, but the M stands for Motivation. Sometimes, trainers teach that the M stands for the Message, as in the message you want to deliver. Those trainers are rightly making the point that the "Message" must be tailored to what you learn in the "F O R." As for me, I tend to delay the "Message" longer than most salesmen. I want to *really* dig in and get to know my new friend, not jump on the sale too soon. Sometimes I even delay the "Message" until the next conversation or the one after that, or the one after that, just because I want to be sure I am really getting to know my new buddy and not being "that" person who just wants to score a sale. I am also waiting until I establish trust and credibility with the new friend. It is still true that people don't care what you know until they know that you care. By the time I'm willing to talk about me, the person is usually asking to know what I know.

You want to ask questions in clever, likeable ways, *not* just peppering your person like a machine gun full of questions. Remember humor makes you very likeable and you win instant credibility. That little tip isn't fair, but it is true. People like funny people, and people like people who are like they are. So, lighten up with this whole process!

It's nearly impossible to guide you on exactly how long to wait on the "Message." Let your intuition be your guide. This goes back to the concept that "sales is an art." You will make mistakes; we all do. Shrug them off, learn the lesson, and keep going. I take time every day to assess how my sales interactions went that day and to learn and grow.

I once enrolled a new friend at a park a week after we first met. Our children were playing happily together, and we were chatting about mom stuff. We had a lot in common due to similar issues with our children. I don't recall how oils came up, but I know that when they did, she announced that she had once called a friend of hers to ask a question about supporting her special needs son, and when she did, *the friend just tried to sell her oils and "didn't really care."* Emphasis MINE.

A week later, this new friend got a starter bundle with me. She didn't want anything to do with being "under that other woman," no matter how I tried to get her to go back and enroll with her friend. I'm sure the friend meant well, and I feel a little bad for her. However, this might be the lesson that friend needed to learn. Do you see the importance of timing and technique?

Because of experiences like this, I have learned that when I finally do get around to presenting the "Message," I tend to lead with *everything but* oils. But that . . . could be a whole *other* book.

GET THEM TALKING

Want to be the most engaging, popular person ever? Want to know how to fill the need? Want to know what to put in your presentation? Want to know exactly how to close? Learn how to get people talking. Here are some of my favorite techniques that have saved my tail when my mind went blank, and I couldn't think of a single thing to ask or say.

These techniques have the effect of a conversational "double click." I want you to picture yourself scrolling through a website. When you find a topic you want to know more about, you simply "double click," and the word becomes a paragraph.

There are three techniques that you can weave throughout your conversation that will encourage people to elaborate right into "letting them have *your* way," and, at the same time, make you ridiculously interesting to those around you.

The first way to get people talking is to simply to say, "tell me more about that." Isn't that simple and amazing? It keeps people talking!
It sounds like this:

> **Me:** *So, do you have babies or fur babies or both?*
> **New Friend:** *Oooh! I have four boys and two dogs!*

Me: *Wow! Tell me more about that!*
New Friend: *"Oh, you wouldn't believe it! We weren't trying for a girl. We just like kids, but I had no idea what boys were like! All my friends had little girls, and I just thought I must be doing something wrong because they wrestle all the time and never sit still and getting them to go to bed is impossible but my husband says he was just the same way, and I wouldn't have it any other way, but I mean, it really kicks up my anxiety when they're always climbing trees so high. Like, we are always in the doctor's office for something. I thought about having more, but I had a rough pregnancy and was absolutely exhausted the whole time, so I don't know . . .*

Okay, students . . . How many "needs" did you just see in that paragraph from *one* question and *double click*? Let's see: fidgety kids, bed time needs, supporting children's systems with NingXia Red®, vitamins, Unwind™, hormone support, mom's wellness cabinet for tree climbing, anxious feelings, pregnancy support, and energy, not to mention the business opportunity.

The second technique to get people talking, I call "Identify." Try these phrases on for size.
"It sounds like" - "It feels like" - "It looks like"

Once you have them talking, notice what they are really saying and then "identify" it.
Example:

They say: *"Oh, I'm so busy running the kids all over the place."*
You say: *"It seems like your family is important*

> *to you."* (Shut up and let them talk.)
> **They say:** *"They are. I've got three kids, and I just want them to have a good childhood. I mean, I remember how much I loved sports, so I don't mind running them places five days a week. It's just the cost of all this is high, but it's worth it."*
> **You say:** *"It sounds like you're willing to pay for what is important to you."* (Shut up and let them talk.)

With just a few words, you can keep them talking, but even more important than that, when you use the "Identify" technique, you cause people to think about what is important to them and how they really feel.

Another benefit is you also validate people's feelings. According to Chris Voss, master negotiator, when negative feelings are validated, they *decrease*. When positive feelings are validated, they *increase*. Win/Win.

Third, is my favorite technique of all time. Echo what they say. No, seriously, echo. Whatever the last three words were (or as you grow your skill set, any words they used), simply repeat with a question in your voice.
Example:

> **They say:** *"Wow, I wish I could win the lottery."*
> **You say:** *"Win the lottery?"*
> **They say:** *"Yes! Oh, man, I would pay off my house. I would tell my boss where to go. I would travel the world. I would take care of my elderly parents. I would start a new business . . ."*

So now you know they want financial security, adventure, travel, freedom, and the comfort of knowing their family is

cared for. To keep them talking, pick any one of those and echo again.
You say: *"Travel?"*
... or *"Pay off your house?"*
... or *"Your elderly parents?*
... or *"Your boss?"*
... and they will talk and talk and talk. **Cue the fireworks.**

Do you see how it happens if you continue on this path for just a few minutes? You may learn *everything* you need to know about that person to find and fill their needs and, when the time comes, to "close them." Moreover, more often than not, they talk themselves right into your plan for them and believe it was their idea all along.

Expert Tip: Echo is an excellent technique to use when someone throws you the old "these oils are too expensive" objection. You say, "too expensive"? and go from there.

All these years later, I have gotten quite good at asking questions and getting to know people. We could be anywhere... the post office, Lowe's, or a garden center and on the way home, Ron will say, "Did that woman seriously just open up and tell you about her hormones, weight gain, hysterectomy, aging parents, and how she can't sleep?"

"Yup." (Big grin)

HAVE A CATCH?

We've learned that skillful salesmen control the flow of a conversation so they can locate the need and to avoid doing all the talking. "Catching" the ball is when you reply to someone's question, either by answering it or by commenting on their answer. "Throwing" the ball is when you ask a question of your own. So, with that visual in your mind, let's make some magic.

Remember, he who asks the questions is in charge of the conversation. Let me say that again for the people in the back.

He who asks the questions is in charge of the conversation.

NOT he who talks; he who asks the questions. If you learn nothing else from this chapter, remember that.

Let's take you back to the Uber driver at the Young Living® Convention. If you're clever, you've thought ahead and are ready with a question, but some drivers are tricky; they get in there first. So, suppose you hop into the back, and before you can think of a question to ask, the driver throws you the ball.

"So, are you in town for convention?"

This moment is where too many brand partners go wrong. There are two ways to blow this. The first way is "catch and drop." If you pause, you drop the ball.

Uber Driver: *"So, are you in town for convention?"*
You: *"Yes!"*
(Pause-Dropped the ball.)
Uber Driver: *"Is this your first trip here?"*
You: *"No! I came last year!*

(Pause-Dropped the ball.)

Do you see the missed opportunity? Besides that, it looks like you're not so interested in conversation, doesn't it? The second way to mess this up is to "Catch and Hold."

Uber: *"So, are you in town for convention?"*

You: "Yes! And this town is really nice! You may have heard of Young Living, we have the Seed to Seal, and our Sourcing, Science and Standards, and of course Gary Young the founder and the story of how he learned about oils and we have farms all over the world and we're so much better than that other company and I have an incredible story that you wouldn't believe and my kids never slept until oils and the oils have made such a big difference in our lives and I do this as a business now and I'm actually an Executive and HERE'S MY CARD!

Somewhere in a galaxy far, far away there is a poor forlorn Uber driver, trying to be nice, with 35 business cards stacked in the center console, and a poor naïve YL rep, thinking the driver is actually going to call her back.

Are you sensing the problem? You just lost control, and you have no idea what makes this person tick. Sometimes the other person throws the ball back and tries to steer the conversation in their direction.

Uber Driver: *"Hi! Are you in town for convention?"*
You: *"I sure am! How long have you been driving Uber?"*
Uber Driver: *"Three months. Do you do this for a business?"*
You: *"I do! What do you love about driving for Uber?"*

You know . . . conversation! They may keep trying to turn the conversation to you, but now you know the rest of the story, and you won't fall for it.

Now, imagine the difference if you are asking the questions.

> **Uber Driver:** *"So, are you in town for convention?"*
>
> **You:** *"I AM in town for convention, and what a friendly city this is!"* (Catch) then without taking a breath, you continue, *"How long have you lived here?"* (Throw)

Followed by other questions . . .

> *"Nice! (Catch) (Throw) Have you been doing this long?"*
>
> *"Wow, Since the beginning!* (Catch) (Throw) *Is this your full-time gig or a side gig??"*
>
> *"Ah.* (Catch) (Throw) *What do you love about it?"*
>
> *"So you're a people person then . . .* (Catch) (Throw) *What do you not like about it?"*
>
> *"Aaah . . .* (Catch) (Throw) *Why do you do it? Nobody just works 80 hours a week for nothing. What is your goal? What's your dream?"*

I could go on forever. Do you see the *difference*? Can you *feel* the difference? Do you see the power of questions and how quickly you can develop a relationship, find the need, and sometimes even close the sale right now? Can you see how this applies to any and all situations? When you play ball, you don't hog the ball.

You asking the questions in the right direction changes everything. Sometimes people try to be polite and turn the questions back on me, with a well-placed, "but tell me about you," but I'm not having it. I reply, "Nah. I'm boring. Back to you!"

Any nuggets I drop here and there are for the purpose of building trust and credibility, and when we get to the point that I finally talk a little about myself, I know exactly what to say. I know how to make the presentation. But that . . . is also a book for another time.

Note that I was using the example of the Uber Driver because that's the story I began with, but this question-asking technique is obviously applicable anywhere there are people.

People ask me, "Well, does it work every time?" Heavens no. But it doesn't have to work every time. What harm does it do you to just get to know people? You're stuck in the car anyway. You're checking out anyway. You're having your hair done anyway. You're at the park anyway. You're in the study group anyway. You're at the pool anyway. You're at the play group anyway. You're at the neighbor's house anyway. Or better yet, you're having the neighbor over anyway. Living life doesn't mean you have to stop working. The BEST thing about not being in a J O B is that your business fits into your life, not the other way around.

So, as you are going about your life seeing and meeting people, train yourself to become aware. You have different goals for different circumstances. Let's take a look at a few.

COLD MARKET IN-PERSON

The primary goals in a cold market are:

To determine if this person is someone you want in your organization. My standards for "customer" are different than for "brand partner." After all, everyone needs Young Living®. I will "sell" oils to anyone with a need. But if I'm going to invest my time and energy in a potential brand partner, my standards are very high because there is only so much time in the world. I believe everyone can meet these high standards, but not everyone is there yet, and that's OK. Is this someone I want to link arms with all the way to the top? Are they friendly? Likeable? Positive? If you're going to work with someone the rest of your life, you want to work with people you enjoy. So, if they don't pass the "gut" test (where my gut likes them) then I tend to pass on them.

To build trust and credibility, be just interesting enough that they want to get to know you more.

Find a connection and a reason to further the conversation. Do you have similar interests or similar circumstances? You may have information they need on another topic. What conversation? ANY conversation! Find a reason to connect on social media or exchange numbers. It sounds like this, "Hey! You're fun! Are you on Insta?" or "Sure! Let me send you my favorite video about homeschooling. What's your number?"

This is not to say that you can't occasionally close people on the spot when you uncover a need and they are ready. Obviously, I've done that. It's just to say that your primary goal is simply to move people from your cold market to an ever-expanding lukewarm market.

LUKEWARM MARKET

The goal of the lukewarm market is to warm up the relationship. You want to reconnect and bond, kindle or re-kindle the friendship. You want to build trust and credibility and find a reason to keep in touch.

It sounds like this, "I've missed you, and we have so much in common. We should re-connect." Or "You know, our kids have always had so much fun together. Would you all like to come over to play someday soon?" Or "I remember working with you all those years ago, and I've always respected how you . . . (name it). Would you have a lunch hour open sometime soon? I'd like to catch up."

WARM AND HOT MARKET

The goal when dealing with the warm and hot market is to find the need and fill it. Have coffee? Talk oils. Go to the soccer match? Talk oils. Find the need and fill it. That's it. Sometimes it's really easy. You're sitting at the soccer tournament and somebody suddenly has a need and you toss her a bottle. She wants more. Send the link. Boom!

WHAT'S NEXT?

As people talk, they will eventually tell you their pain and their need. While I will sometimes close on the spot (if the timing is right) with my flip kit, usually what I'm "selling" is a version of an invitation, a tool, a presentation, a story, a sample (or anointing), or a scan.

> *"If I sent you a short video, would you watch it and tell me what you think?"*
>
> *"Would you like to come to my community zoom meeting? You'll love the other ladies!"*
>
> *"A group of us young moms meets every Wednesday at my house. Want to come?"*

"Hey! I've got a group on social media where we talk about this stuff all the time. Want me to pop you in there?"
"I teach classes on Tuesdays. You must come."
"Can I tell you a story?" (Yours or someone else's! Facts tell; stories sell.)
"Have you ever heard of a ZYTO scan?"
"Yikes! Here! Want to try this?"

Let's talk about presentations for a moment. When you hear "Presentation," what comes to mind; you standing in front of a group talking? Yes, but also simply telling a story. Generally, I define "presentation" this way: any time you are talking, be it one sentence or a day-long lecture, whether to one person or a stadium full of listeners in rapt attention.

Presenting, therefore, can and must be tailored and pithy. There are many ways to "present."

Building Trust and Credibility (keep it short!)
Educating/Inspiring
Answering questions, both spoken and unspoken
Telling targeted stories
Establishing Common Ground

Use your words wisely. Use fewer words. Be short and concise.

Big Pointola: Make sure you "pocket" any needs you uncover as you're asking questions. File them in the back of your mind. If you invited them to a class, bring up those topics while you teach. I call this pressing on the pain point. Your prospect will wonder how it is that you are such a genius mind-reader.

A word about objections: "I can't afford it" or "I'm not interested" or "I have to check with my husband" are all "objections." The term "handling objections" means to help people see past their reasons for saying "no" and bring them over to a "yes." Handling an objection is really just a subset of a presentation. Most salesmen think that you "handle objections" after you close; however, the skilled salesmen anticipate the objections and handle them during the presentation. I call this "speaking the hidden agenda." Do you know your person has a limiting belief? **Handle it** during the presentation and avoid their excuses later! For example, if you suspect someone has a poverty mentality about oils, you could remark during your presentation, "I have saved *so* much money just because I invested in this fantastic set of oils!"

The more you know about your audience, the more powerful and on-target your presentation will be. But that . . . is another book. For now, sit with yourself for a moment and think about common objections you hear. Then, weave the answers into your presentation. **You. Are. Welcome.**

One final thought on this: People ask me all the time, "Is it better to lead with the *product or the business*?" **Buzzer sound!** Wrong question. **You lead with the relationship**, which will tell you which way to go.

Ron and Lori on the 2017 YL cruise

Lori at the Monkey Experience. 2017 YL cruise

Mary and Lori on the 2017 cruise

"Intuition is the number one tool in the toolbox."
~Matthew Mellon

BUYING SIGNALS

But how do I know *when* to close?! Now that you have learned what makes that person tick and uncovered the need(s) and filled the needs, it's time for you to look for the right moment to close, or in *salesman speak,* "buying signals." In Lori speak, it's anything you agree on. It's the other person showing interest. I want you to remember that you are not just selling oils. You are selling the next level of understanding

taking charge of your own wellness
protecting your children
a box of empowerment
a bottle of possibilities
attending a class
community
you.

Some of the biggest examples of "buying signals" are when they say, "I need," "I like," or "I want." I picked up this little gem from Karen Malone, Young Living® Diamond. If you haven't heard of her yet, you will. If you're telling a story and they reply with "I need," "like," or "want," **The time Is NOW** to close!

Here are some examples of buying signals:
They sign up for a free trial/filling out a form, for example at a vendor event.
They ask a question about a product recommendation.
They ask "how it all works."
They ask about price, terms and conditions, obligations, methods of payment, etc.
They want to buy an oil from you.

So, think about this in terms of Young Living®. What are the buying signals to be on the lookout for?
They answer your post about offering to loan out your diffuser.
They like or comment on an oily story.
They ask what oil would "work for" a situation.
They want to know how much an oil is.
They want to know how much a kit is.
They want to know if they "have to sell."
They ask if there are any catches or quotas.
They ask if you can really make money at this.
They ask if they have to buy something every month.
They ask if there is a membership fee.
They want to know why your oils are so "expensive."
They say, "Wow! That sounds wonderful! I want to feel that good too!"
They say, "I need to feel better!"
They remark, "I like that smell!"

We will handle how to close shortly, but can you see how watching for the right moment just got a little easier?

A QUICK WORD ABOUT CLOSING

When you hear "close," what comes to mind? Some people think of a "close" as the question you ask at the end of a class. Yes, it certainly is that, but it's also so much more. Any time you are asking someone to make a decision or agree to a concept, you are "closing." So, by this definition, any "invitation," whether it's to a class or to try a sample or to watch a documentary or to "grab their oils" or to link arms and run to Royal Crown Diamond is a "close." Basically, everything you say is either a question, a presentation, or a close.

So, in other words, it could go like this:
Ask Questions
Present
Close
Handle Objections

But in reality, it often goes like this:
Ask questions
Ask questions
Ask questions
Present -Handle Objections
Present -Handle Objections
Close
Ask questions
Present – Build Credibility
Close
Handle Objections
Close
Handle Objections
Close
Ask Questions
Present- Close

Meaning . . . it's messy. It's not a formula. It's different for everyone. Remember, this is an art *and* a science, and your intuition will be your guide.

How can there be multiple closes? Remember the definition of "close." You are helping someone to say "yes" to a concept. You are helping them to say "yes" to the next concept. Some call it "the nudge."

If you imagine a scale from one to a hundred where one is "I have zero interest in essential oils or clean makeup or nutritional products or in living a better life at all" and 100 is "I want to run to Royal Crown Diamond with you!" your goal is *not* to take someone from one to one hundred in this one interaction. It is to take them from 1 to 2. Or from 10 to 11. Or from 79 to 80. Or, sometimes, from 25 to 30. There is only so much truth people are ready to hear at once. Eventually with time and skill, you may be able to guide them all the way to 100.

Remember, too, you attract people based upon the number (or level of awareness) that you are. You do not attract who you *want*. You attract who you *are*. People like people who are like they are, and you cannot lead people to a place you have not been. Combine that concept with the power of social media, and you have the opportunity to grow very quickly. But that is also a book for another time. Since I did not grow mainly on social media, I must first hone that skill before attempting to teach it. I would, however, imagine that all these skills are applicable when you're dealing with people online because, after all, they are people. I have used these skills myself to enroll a few dozen strangers off social media, so I know they work.

So, having said that:
What are you selling to the person who loves their plug-ins and their candles and disinfectant spray? ***Watch the movie Stink.***

What are you selling to the person who is wary of chemicals but is using the typical greenwashed products? ***Do some research, try some Thieves® Household Cleaner, or come to a class.***

What are you selling to the person who is using "essential oils" from Walmart? ***Quality matters. Do some research. Try ours. Maybe visit a farm.***

What are you selling to the person who is interested in oils but doesn't have time to come to a class? ***Watch a presentation.***

What are you selling to the mom who may be lonely and doesn't have any crunchy friends? ***Community.***

What are you selling to the person who takes good care of her children but doesn't want to take care of herself? ***You are worth it.***

What are you selling to a person who is terrified of germs? ***Terrain Theory.***

What are you selling to the person who is into herbs? ***The power of an essential oil.***

What are you selling to the person who wants to buy a bottle of lavender? ***Subscribe and Save to unlock the 24% and come to a class.***

What are you selling to the person who wants a bundle? ***Get on Loyalty Rewards.***

What are you selling to the person who is on Loyalty Rewards? ***Educate yourself and consider grabbing your builder bundle.***

What are you selling to the Executive? ***Silver.*** What are you selling to the Silver? ***Gold . . . all the way up to Royal Crown Diamond.***

You do not attract who you want.

You attract who you are.

Race to the Finish Hawaii trip 2018

Ron and Lori at Race to the Finish in Hawaii 2018

Global Leadership cruise to Alaska 2019

ON THE CAKE

"Do not wait; the time will never be 'just right'. Start where you stand, and work with whatever tools you may have at your command, and better tools will be found as you go along."
~George Herbert

Join me for a little tour around the kitchen where we talk about several seemingly random tips and techniques. Oh, yes! Finally! The tips and techniques, baby!

COLOR PERSONALITY

You may have noticed me referencing people according to their "color" (Red, Yellow, Green, and Blue). If you have no idea what I'm talking about, you can take a color personality test by searching for jacobadamo.com.

Knowing yourself is key to knowing others, and there are many ways to understand personalities from "Myer's Briggs" to "Enneagram." Because the "color" test is so popular among Young Living® Brand Partners, I often refer to it. I like it because it is very, very simple and helps people begin to have a good basic understanding of how they "tick" so they can be the best version of themselves.

UPGRADE YOUR LANGUAGE

Times have changed and language has shifted. Nobody likes an MLM. No really, a few of us who really understand the concept love it, but there's no sense in using language that is polarizing. Words create emotion and paint pictures, so choose them carefully. Consider ditching and switching your lingo to be more winsome. More nonchalant. Lighter.

Instead of **Member** try **Customer and "unlock the 24%."**
Instead of **Distributor/Business Builder** try **Brand Partner.**
Instead of **Starter Kit** try **Starter bundle** or just **"set."**
Instead of **Autoship** try **Subscription Service.**
Instead of **Build a business** try **Use your referral code/link or generate an income.**
Instead of **Party** or **Class** try **Get Together.** (Sometimes I purposely use "class," depending on my audience.)

Your goal is to make things sound and feel easy, simple, delightful, normal or even classy or upscale. It will save you from having to backpedal and explain away the image you created with the MLM-speak.

LOANER KITS

The story goes that once there was a pet shop that was having trouble selling puppies, so they decided to change their policy. No longer would the customer be required to purchase the dog. Rather, if someone expressed an interest, they were encouraged to "take the dog home" and bring it back in a month if the dog was unwanted. As you can imagine, hardly anyone brought the dog back. This technique became known as the, you guessed it, "Take the Dog Home" sales technique.

So, what does that look like? You simply ask if the person would like to borrow your diffuser and some oils. This is especially effective if you see someone express a need. Tell them the only thing you ask is that they use the diffuser every night for a week or two, and then give it back, along with a review of how they liked it. The short answer is most people don't want to give it back; they want to keep it or buy their own.

NOTE: It should be obvious, but I want to say it to be sure . . . I don't support puppy mills, but I can't control the name of the sales technique. It is what it is.

FLIP KIT

A flip kit is a new Starter Bundle that you keep in your possession to give to the person you are referring, so they don't have to wait on their kit to arrive. The way to make it happen is to hand your bundle to the new member and send their newly purchased bundle to your address.

People are *much* more likely to purchase if they can have it immediately, especially in non-US markets. It's much more tangible. Let's take a look at the psychology of the sale.

I cannot tell you how many times I have closed somebody just because I had a complete kit of oils in my car. The reason you want to have the kit in the car is because you want to do it now.

NOW

NOW

NOW

NOW

NOW, while the purchase still feels like a good idea.

Let me talk you through what is sometimes happening psychologically. I learned this concept of the terror barrier from Bob Proctor.

When I refer to the conscious mind, I mean the part of your mind that includes all the thoughts you are aware you have. When I refer to the subconscious mind, I mean the part of your mind that runs automatically without you being *aware.* It demonstrates the thoughts and ideas that you *really* believe, without even having to think about it. It drives most of your behavior and discloses what you believe at the core of your being, whether or not those beliefs match with your conscious thoughts. All those thoughts you've internalized your entire life that now make up your belief system are stored in your subconscious.

So, the scene is set. Your prospect begins to realize this set of oils is so much more than just oils, and they begin to actually . . . *BELIEVE.*

That belief is in the conscious mind, and it sounds like this:

> *"Oooh! Maybe there's a better way! I could get this bundle of oils! It's only $165! I could kick all the toxic chemicals out, maybe sleep a little better, help my little ones go to bed, be a little happier, maybe share oils with a few other people . . . I think maybe I could actually do this! I think I'm going to do this! I am! I am going to DO this!"*

But it isn't what their subconscious mind believes, and cognitive dissonance kicks in, leading to absolute bedlam inside their mind. (This is also the psychology of buyer's remorse.) The subconscious comes out, and starts screaming . . .

> *"Who do you think you are??? Have you lost your mind??? Nothing ever goes right for you! This might be for someone else, but it isn't for you!*

> *Have there ever been any double-blind placebo studies to prove it's safe??? It isn't approved by any three-letter government agency! Your husband is going to kill you if you spend that money! People will think you're crazy! What if the car breaks down or the water heater goes out??? You don't know anybody! You can't sell anything! You may be broke, but at least you have your integrity! Have you lost your mind????"*

And you can see them bounce right off that terror barrier. Of course, they don't say all that. What they say is, "Ummmm, le . . . mmeeee . . . *think* about it" with a blank look on their face.

Know that sometimes, when you have that beautiful bundle right there, people are able to overcome their negative paradigms for a short time, get caught up in hope, make a decision, and grab their kit! But if you don't have the oils right there, it sounds like this:

> *"Ooooh, you don't have any right here? That's OK. No worries! I'll do it tomorrow! Just call me tomorrow!"*

. . . And then, when you call the next day, their phone number has been disconnected. You're going to have to skip trace them. They went witness protection on you because the moment they got "out of it," they got the psychological "let down."

> *"Oh, PHEW!* (wipes brow) *Oh, have mercy. I almost did it! I almost wasted $165! My husband would have killed me! I'm sure there's nothing to it. I mean, if it worked, my doctor would be using it. I already spent all that money on those*

> *candles anyway. I'll just grab that set I saw at the Sam's club. The car payment is coming up and the water heater is on its last leg. Besides that, I'd rather have a "real" job than do some stupid pyramid scheme. I mean, I may not have much money, but at least I'm not that person. (Catches breath) Ohmywordno. She's going to try to call me tomorrow!!! Noooooo! I just won't answer. Maybe I'll get a burner and cancel my phone! Well, I'm not answering! NO WAY."*

Because psychologically, for some people, sick is *comfortable* and broke feels *normal.*

I mentioned before how many times I have enrolled someone because I had a flip kit in my car. (This is not unique to me; this is common in Young Living®.) Recently, I was in Hawaii because I earned the Dream 1000 trip. Of course, I brought a flip kit with me . . . all the way to Hawaii. Another member saw it and said, "What did you bring that for?" Deadpan, I replied, "be . . . cause I'm gonna flip it." . . . and, I did.

BUSY BUSY BUSY

Successful people are busy. You are successful. You are busy. One of the best phrases you can memorize is, "I am on a short leash just now" or "I don't have the time just now" or "I can't chat now," but I do want to talk with you about this. Can we talk next Tuesday?" Remember, friend, people buy *you*. They don't want to go with someone who has all the time in the world because they perceive that person must not be very much in demand. Sometimes playing "hard to get" works out to your advantage, and if you do this right, you won't have to play "hard to get" very long, as you will actually be "hard to get!"

CONFIDENCE and WIIFM

When purchasing, people are always asking themselves, "What's in it for me?" (WIIFM) So in all your dealings, be sure to express the ideas from the perspective of the buyer.

> *"I happen to have one in my car. You can have it if you need it to get started now. I don't mind."* (WIIFM)

> *"If it would help, I could come to your house. Just grab a few friends and we'll sit around your kitchen table and I'll teach them about oils."* (WIIFM)

Now keep that concept in mind and unite it with this. **People buy confidence.** In fact, researchers have consistently found a correlation between confidence and success. I hear too many people slink into an invitation from a wimpy, feeble, self-centered, pity place.

> *"Heeeyyyy, I'm having a class, would you pleeease come? It would mean so much to me because I'm trying to do this business and I'm not getting a lot of people and . . . "*

Ick, right? It feels a little pathetic, and nobody enrolls with pathetic. Well, they sometimes do, but that's not the vibe you want. I'm not saying you can't ever do the casual, nonchalant invitation from out of the blue. That sounds like this:

> *"Hey! I'm having a class on Thursday. I don't know if you'd be interested, but if you are, I'd love to have ya!"*

Or,

> *"Hey! I'm having an oil thing on Monday with some of my other friends, and I don't know if you'd be interested, but I thought maybe you would, so I thought I'd ask. We will have a little snack thing, and we'll have a lot of fun! Would you want to come?"*

In fact, that invitation, if done correctly, can be very effective. It still assumes that the benefit of coming belongs to the prospect, not the hostess.

Maybe now is the best time to gently address the "I've been challenged to sell five starter bundles before the end of the month. Help me reach my goal" posts that I see. Wellll . . . I want to be delicate because I'm super proud of that person for posting anything. I'm super happy they want to change lives. But do you see the self-centered nature of that post? A sympathy purchase does not typically a life-long user make.

"But Lorrriiii, I've got goooaaaals." Yes, I know you do, and I'm happy for that! So, let's have high expectations for your level of work and low expectations for what people do *for you*. We can adjust that message with "WIIFM" in mind.

> *"Well, friends, I'm up on a big goal, so that means I'm willing to do things I don't normally do, which puts you in the cat bird position, you lucky, lucky duck!"* Then you make your offer. *"If you enroll today, I'll give you* (whatever the policies and procedures allow). *Get in now because the kids are going to bed, and I don't have all day to wait!"*

HUMOR AND THE LIKEABILITY FACTOR

This little topic, in and of itself, could be an entire book. As you see, I have mentioned humor several times already. **People buy from people they like**, and people like people who make them laugh or chuckle. Don't force it, but if you are a collector of humor and can throw in a little quip, it relaxes people and makes them feel good. And making other people feel good makes you feel good, doesn't it?

When people *like* you, they subconsciously assign you positive attributes in their minds and hearts. It's similar to how people feel about those whose accents they enjoy. They just think the best of you, much like I assume anyone with a foreign accent is a genius. If you have a French or a British accent, you can just come sit down and read me a phone book. See what I did there?

So, how do you get funnier? Well first of all, lighten up a little. Don't take yourself so seriously. Learn to laugh at you. Next, go on YouTube and watch funny videos. No,

I'm not kidding. Remember, you are the sum total of the five people you hang around. Spend some time hanging around funny people. It may change your perspective on life and help you to see the gentle humor all around you. Third, read good books. The best book on the topic ever written is *How to Win Friends and Influence People.* Read it, read it, read it.

One final note on this topic: stick with the AT&T principle of humor – keep it appropriate, timely, and tasteful. Nobody likes people who make jokes at other's expense. Well, there are people who like them, but those aren't typically the most successful network marketers and probably not the people you want to do business with.

MIRRORING

People like people who are like they are, and remember, people don't really buy oils; they buy you. Mirroring is an advanced technique, oh, but friend . . . if you will use it, you will up your game dramatically. ***REDS***, I'm talking to you. Sometimes reds do things their way, rather than anyone else's way, just because they think their way is better. But reds also like success, so there's that. And true reds understand relationship. They understand that he who serves the most people . . . wins.

If you want to form relationship with anyone, watch them. Study them, and mirror them. Mirroring is where you subtly adopt, mimic, or match the other person's posture, gestures, speech patterns and volume, mannerisms, attitudes, voice tone, facial expressions, and body language. You see mothers and babies do this intuitively. Most of us do this subconsciously with people we like. Moreover, some of this is so powerful, it's unavoidable. Why do you yawn when others yawn?

Observe close friends talking, and you will see it. They both lean in, or they both lean out, or they both cross their arms and legs, or they both sit with their hands folded, or they both walk with their jackets over their shoulders (this is common with men). When you open your eyes to this, you will notice it everywhere you go. Mirroring creates empathy.

Generally, but not always, people in the southern states speak more slowly. They think fast talkers are tricky. People in northern states, especially on the east coast, speak very quickly. They sometimes think slow talkers are slow thinkers. We are all making subtle decisions and judgments every day that we aren't even aware we are making. It's not fair. It just is what it is.

Someone once said this technique is manipulative. Let me gently address that. There are toxic, narcissistic, abusive people who have mastered this skill and use it for their own nefarious intent. I know because . . . I know. They also use the skill of "love bombing." Just because they show false love, should we then not love one another in a genuine way? Of course not. What some use for wickedness, others use for good. The fact that some people are horribly manipulative does not mean that the rest of us cannot simply build some rapport. MmmmKay? You see, there's another group of people who mirror naturally, with hardly a thought. They are the empaths.

According to pacesconnection.com, researchers have discovered a specialized group of brain cells that are responsible for compassion. These cells enable everyone to mirror emotions, to share another person's pain, fear, or joy. Because empaths are thought to have hyper-responsive mirror neurons, we deeply resonate with other people's feelings. Simply put, mirror neurons allow us to imitate others. Those who have more, or more responsive mirror neurons, imitate more.

Mirror neurons at work with my daddy and my son

I can also testify that as someone growing up in a family with deaf grandparents, I read body language like a native speaker speaks his first language. My assumption is that I have good mirror neurons because my father was a child of deaf parents and because mannerisms, facial expressions, and body language were fluently spoken in our home.

This technique, therefore, is not intended to be used to manipulate, but to serve. People receive information better when it is delivered for them, not how you prefer to say it. They don't have to translate the message when it is delivered in their native "language."

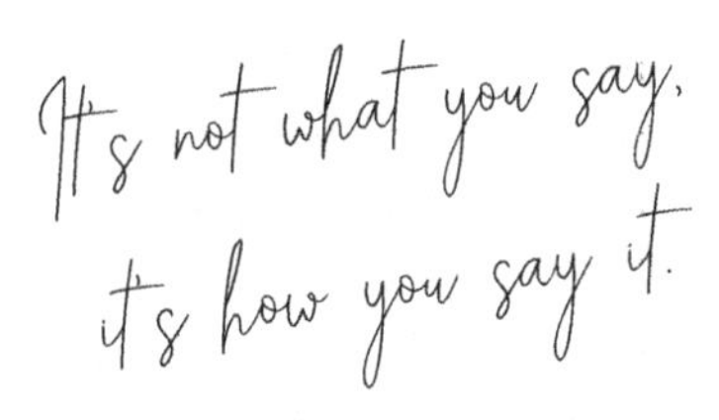

When I was a consultant, it was common for my clients to remark to me, "We're the same type, aren't we?" I usually chuckled and said, "I'm sure of it!" The reason they thought that is because I had learned to mirror my clients to the extent that my body language, voice tone, presentations, written reports, emails, and phone calls were all designed to deliver content in the way that best served my client. (They were referring to the Myers Briggs Type Indicator, which is something you should search and learn about. I speak ENFP, for the record. They call us . . . "the chameleon.")

You can use your mirror neurons to:

Bond with people
"Read" a room
Tailor a presentation
Close the sale
Handle Objections

It's not what you say, it's how you say it. Let me give you a few examples of handling objections using mirroring. Because this is in print, I ask you to imagine different voice tones and body languages . . .

(Soft spoken, not gregarious, unsure, looking down)
They say: *"Sigh . . . well, I dunno. It seems like a lot of money."*

You say: *"Sigh . . . well, I know, but you can save a ton of money too, and if it doesn't work, you can get your money back."*

(Shy, giggly, youngish)
They say: Giggle . . . *"OHMYGOSH my husband would kill me . . . "*
You say: Giggle . . . *"OHMYGOSH. WAIT till you break out that ONE oil tonight just for him!!!"*

(Firm, no-nonsense, confident, blank faced)
They say: *"Well. I'm someone who likes to do my research. I don't make snap decisions."*
You say: *"Well. The best way to research is to ask your body. So, I'd recommend you take the next step."*
(Frustrated, semi-angry, half-yelling)
They say: *"I'M SICK OF FEELING LIKE THIS! I DON'T WANNA BE SICK AND TIRED ANYMORE! "*
You say: *"I TELL YOU WHAT YOU'RE GONNA DO. YOU'RE GONNA SNAG THAT BUNDLE, PLUG IN THAT DIFFUSER, AND HAVE THE BEST NIGHT'S SLEEP OF YOUR LIFE!"*

SITUATIONAL AWARENESS AND ATTITUDE

As an *independent* distributor, how you run your business is up to you (within the bounds of the policies and procedures). There are many subtle decisions to be made along the way about what your business will look like, so it helps to think some situations through before they happen. I am reminded of the proverb that reads, "All is permissible, but not all is profitable," or as the knight in *Indiana Jones and the Last Crusade* gravely warned, "You must choose, but choose wisely."

The question that used to strike terror into the heart of even the most intrepid YL entrepreneurs was some form of "I don't want the starter kit. I just want one oil." This question alone stopped many brand partners from success because they simply didn't know how to navigate this incredible opportunity. Here are some situations you may have encountered where this objection came up.

There you were, sitting at the soccer match, oiling up with your Valor®, and another mom said, "Mmmm. That smells amazing. Can I get some?" (Remember how the blood used to drain from your face as you began this awkward little tap dance? "Nooooo . . . you don't actually want a bottle of Valor®! What you want is a $185 bundle of oils (after tax and shipping), including the Valor®, or at least you want a $35 box of Stress Away™ (you'll love it, trust me), a few NingXia Red® packets, mints, hand sanitizer, *plus* the Valor®!" Then, there's the time your neighbor called and said, "Hey! I love that Thieves® cleaner you gave me. Can you order me some?" Other times, it was an objection to grabbing their own account. They didn't want to be bothered and would rather "just get it from you."

Or the most devastating of all, when you have poured your heart and soul out in a class, explaining all the life changing aspects of the magical bundle of oils, complete with rainbows and lollipops, only to be dashed to bits when your prospect said, "I don't want the whole bundle. I just want the peppermint." (Cue dark music)

Remember? Ah, yes . . . this one question held so many brand partners back. BUT NO MORE! Since Young Living® upgraded their system to make way for a truly customized oily beginning, we are allowed to meet people precisely where they are. Gone are the days when everyone had to be funneled into only a few ways to get started. People can make an account with as little as a lip balm! The impact of this subtle enhancement cannot be overstated. This feature is so good, that I called Marcella and emphatically told her it was so easy to enroll people that my book was not necessary, and I wasn't going to publish. She set me straight, as only Vonn can do, and so, you have this book in your hands today.

Let's take a look at these opportunities with new eyes! First of all, your willing, helpful, "can do" opportunity-driven attitude will drive you to make any of these situations work out perfectly.

Consider the soccer mom who wants the Valor® or the neighbor who calls to ask for more of that plant-based cleaner that smells like Christmas (after you gave her a little bottle as part of a housewarming gift, you clever, clever gal) or even the attendee at a class who insists she would never use any of the oils except peppermint. The new answer can be a breezy, "Shoot yeah! Let me send you a link. Be sure to click subscribe to save so you get the 24% discount!"

But Lori, shouldn't we have the bigger conversation with them and ask them about their needs and create a custom package and tell them all their options, like you said to do? Well, yes of course, if they are open to it in the moment. But don't overcomplicate things. Not everyone wants all the ins and outs of 800 products and purchase opportunities presented to them in the middle of a tight soccer match. They just want that sweet smelling Valor® you just used, so get them set up with their bottle of oil and *then* educate them!

The education must happen either way. The only question is *when* it will happen. When all roads led to the $165 kit, a great bit of education had to happen before the purchase point. Now, it can happen whenever the customer is prepared to receive it, before, during, and/or after the purchase.

I firmly believe the best way to get started is with a bundle or assortment of products that people can use and play with and get to know and fall in love with, especially now that you can custom-build bundles, based upon their needs. However, if that isn't their path, don't push it. Sometimes people have to fall in love with the Thieves® Household Cleaner (or the Vitality Drops™, or the Progessence Plus™, or the supplements) before they are willing to even take a look at other products.

Because it is so simple to help people get access to YL oils, the temptation will be to stop there. Please hear my admonition. After they have their account, the real work begins! Follow up, follow up, follow up and educate, educate, educate. Do **not** just figure that once your friend is a customer, you've done your job. No matter what they start with, but especially if it is a limited number of products, your job to educate and inspire them to embrace the lifestyle. Be sure to get them into classes and, as Mary says, sit around the kitchen table and tell them what these oils *really* do.

"Sure! Here's my link, and the next time I have a class, you've just gotta be there so you can _____ (feed their words back to them)."

Side note to those who have extra oils in their stash and are tempted to trade them for immediate cash: Please do ***not*** suggest that you sell someone "one of yours" because you need the money. Do you realize you are stuck in short term thinking? If someone has to go through you every time they need an oil, they are less likely to take charge of their own wellness. Besides that, you are trading a quick buck for residual income. (Smacks head) *Staaahp!* My answer is to hand the customer the bottle she seeks and say "The way it works is we can set up an account and you order it and just give it back to me when it arrives. That way you can have it now!"

This also goes for members of your downline. If someone three levels down needs an oil from me, my standard answer is to hand them my oil and tell them to put it on order and return the oil to me when it arrives. This protects the OGV and paychecks of my loyal brand partners, rather than pad my wallet with direct sale profits.

Now take the rare person who doesn't want to be bothered setting up an account and insists you order it for them. Consider that if you are at the very beginning of your journey and it's your next-door neighbor who is asking, and it will help you get to your 300 PV point level, then why not serve them and order them a bottle? (Be sure to charge what the policies and procedures require).

But, if the person asking lives an hour away and is expecting you to deliver it like an Avon lady, then that's another consideration. If you say "no," however, say it with grace and a big dose of why that isn't the best for *them*.

I've heard people teach that we should answer with a bit of a haughty spirit, "No. It's not my job to order your oils for you and spend my time traveling around like a door dasher. You need your own account."

Ummmm wow. Why would you even have that attitude with people? I mean, you can say that to people if you wanna, but if you don't want to serve that person, then send them to me because I'll take care of them! You catch a lot more bees with honey, *honey*.

Realize that part of what is going on here is that people are used to how *most* MLMs work. In other companies, not everyone can be a brand partner for $30. Many companies require a buy-in with large orders, quotas, and inventories. I once watched a woman invest $1500 in a pantyhose company that went under 6 months into her journey. *Ouch.* Many reps have the goods piling up in their spare room because the quotas were so high. They are "garage qualified." So, in this world, buying something directly from a distributor benefits the distributor.

That means they may think they are helping *you* when they ask you to just order something for them. They think you're pulling it from your garage. They think of you as their "oily gal" the same way people have their "31 person" or "Avon lady." So, assume the best of people and answer with that in mind. Others may have been burned by other network marketing "book-o-the-month" clubs and are wary. No matter. Your can-do attitude will make it work.

If you say yes, then do it with enthusiasm! "Shoot yeah! Let me grab it on my next order, and I'll sashay on over when it arrives, and we will clean something together!" (Well, you don't actually have to say "sashay." I just sort of threw that in there.)

If you say "no," then do it with class. "The best way to do this is for you to order it off the website so you don't have to rely on me to remember to get it to you because my order doesn't go in until next month and besides that, you know how busy we both are. It's actually easy peasy, and you can do it whenever you want and not be waitin' on me. I'll send you a link. Be sure to put it on subscribe to save to unlock the 24% discount!"

Even still, you may still get some people who push back completely and refuse to make their own account. OK Class. When people put you in this position, what are you "selling?"
Relationship and service
Knowledge and credibility
There's more than they know
You are willing and able to help
Come to a class
Get a real account
and . . .**You are their "oily" person**. Again, you get to decide what to do. Here's my answer: (Godfather voice again) "Sure. I will do this thing for you, but someday, when I have a class, your butt is in the chair." And then, I do it – *once.*

Does this actually work? I've never had anyone say, "no."

Lori Enjoying Hawaii
2020

Hey, Our Names are on the Winner's Wall - 2020

Learning THE CLOSES

"If you don't ask, the answer is always 'no'."
~ Nora Roberts

Here it is . . . Here's the money. All the threads come together to form the sweater with this chapter: ***The Closes!*** Before you jump into this looking for the *one* supernatural, mystical, abracadabra close . . . know that I don't believe it exists. Well, it may exist, but I've never found it. I want you to look at these closes and techniques as tools in your toolbox. When artists use their tools, they know which one to choose, and they wield it with grace. As you practice, you too will gain the intuition to know which close to use, when.

If all you have is a hammer, everything looks like a nail. But, don't let that discourage you! Because I can tell you this: if all I had was a hammer,

I'd hammer in the morning,
I'd hammer in the evening,
all over this land.

(Snort) See what I did there?

The point isn't *what* close you use. The point is to *close*! So, dig in and find one to start with. Choose one that resonates with you. As you gain expertise, you will pick up another and then another. Refer back to this section and re-read it. Practice with your buddy. Memorize a few things so they roll off your tongue. Before you know it, you'll have a plethora of instruments to play with. And ultimately, you will be able to choose the close that is best for the prospect rather than the one that suits you. That, my friends, will be an epic day.

Before we get rolling, I want you to think of how you got started in Young Living®. What close got you in? See if you can find it in the following pages. Here's my story on how I was closed.

I attended a family conference hosted by James and Stacy McDonald a year before I joined up with Young Living®. She was a sweet little thang running around and helping kids do those hippy oils at a craft table. (Recall authenticity, trust, and credibility.)

I don't know if they realize this, but they used a subtle closing technique on me. When I was having a conversation with Stacy, James approached and interrupted. He needed a bottle of peppermint for a headache. I thought it was a little weird, but I tell you what . . . James and Stacy were authentic and trustworthy and had loads of credibility, and they were patient. The following year, I marched up to the oil table and "signed up."

The point isn't what close you use.
The point is to close!

RE-ENGAGING SOMEONE

A lot of people say to me that they don't know how to bring up a topic after they left it without saying what they wanted to say. Nothing could be simpler. "Hey, friend. I've been thinking about our conversation." or "Hey, friend. I've been thinking about you."

Example:

> *"Hey, Becky, I've been thinking about our conversation and how you were telling me about your little one. I'm having a little get together and I don't know if it's something you'd be interested or not, but it might be the answer you've been looking for."*

INVITATION EXAMPLES

Product-focused invitations:

> *"You know, I've been doing a lot of research on all the chemicals in our life and how they are affecting our reproductive systems. I teach classes on it on Tuesday nights. You need this info. Say you'll come."*

> *"It's funny you mentioned that. I teach classes on things like this, and I'm having a little class on Thursday. What do I have to do to get you there?"*

> *"Friend, I've been thinking about our conversation from the other day. You totally need my community. A bunch of us get together on Zoom on Monday nights and talk oils. I don't know if you'd be interested, but I think it just might be the thing you've been looking for. You can totally nurse the baby and watch. You in?"*

"Girl! I just started learning about these oils, and I'm having so much fun! I thought about you. There's this mama group that meets on Thursday afternoons and the kids play and the moms talk crunchy stuff. Wanna come with me?"

"OK . . . All of those are good questions, and I want to do them justice. I'm super covered up right now, and I have to go. Let's get together this week for tea and we can play 'stump the chump.' What day works best for you?"

"Holy cow. You need Thieves®. I'm on my way."

"Hey friend. I saw your post. If I sent you a roller bottle, would you use it?"

"So, after we talked last week, I got to thinking. If I sent you a video, would you watch it? I think it might just have the answer you've been looking for."

BIZ INVITATIONS:

"Hey, Becky. I wanted to reach out to you after our conversation the other day. I'm always looking for people who are team players, self-motivated, and dependable. I don't have time right now, but let's get together to see how you can help pay for your kid's college. What does Monday, at 10, look like for you?"

"Friend . . . I have been where you are (exhausted mom, retail, waitress, side hustle, whatever); it

seems like you are really struggling, and our conversation really touched me. I wouldn't be a good person if I didn't tell you about what I do. I think it could be the answer you've been looking for. When can we talk?"

"Hi friend, I love hearing the stories of how everyone in your office comes by your desk when they need your oils for their daily hit. It's possible that your love of oils could help get your order paid for each month. When can we chat?" (This is when I would follow up with "How about Tuesday?")

"Hi, friend. I know you love your NingXia Red®. If I sent you a short video, would you watch it?"

I BELIEVE

This is the close I used at the beginning of the book to enroll my Uber driver. I learned this close from Marcella Vonn Harting, maybe a day before I tried it out on the Uber driver. Here's how it goes:

"I believe _________.
I believe _________.
I believe _________.

If you believe what I believe, you belong on my team." Or "If you believe what I believe, you need Young Living®." Or "If you believe what I believe, you need this biz." Boom.

Here's the secret sauce to the "I believe" close. The "I believes" can be exactly what your prospect said. You, my friend, are clever enough to pay attention when people talk, pocket the info, and bring it out when the time comes!

In the case of the "tree in the garden" one, I made it up but it was in the same vein as what he had said. The other two "I believes" were the exact statements that he had made during the conversation.

Another magical use of the "I believe" close is to speak life and vision and possibilities into your prospect, to help them envision a better way, to inspire. Observe:

I believe:

> *"We are fearfully and wonderfully made."*
> *"People these days are slaves to the corner stores."*
> *"If you support the body, it knows how to take care of itself."*
> *"In the absence of toxic chemicals, our bodies better maintain homeostasis."*
> *"Our bodies function beautifully."*
> *"These oils are magic in a bottle."*
> *"Most of the diagnosis the doctor gave me were nothing but a collection of symptoms."*
> *"You were designed for more."*
> *"You have a story and a voice that people need to hear."*
> *"We can change the world one person at a time."*
> *"Children need rested mamas."*
> *"It is possible to have it all."*
> *"If you see it in your mind, you can hold it in your hand."*
> *"You don't have to be married to a J O B, making someone else's dreams come true."*
> *"You can afford to take vacation with children if you know how."*
> *"When you serve others, the money chases you."*
> *"You can swap out every toxic chemical in your house and save money doing it."*

"People actually save boatloads of money when they have oils."
"Mothers should be empowered to handle most situations at home."
"There are solutions that come without fear or lab coats or corner stores."
"YOU are the gatekeeper of your home, and YOU decide what crosses the threshold."
"We have compromised our God given intuition."
"We need to be armed with tools for the future."
"We have given away too much of our power."
"The time to dig your well is before you're thirsty."

I could go on all day long, and so could you.

CLOSING LIKE DANI JOHNSON

At the end of the presentation (like a class or a community online meeting), ask your friend,

"What did you like about what you saw/heard?"
"Tell me more about that."
"Great! How do you want to take care of this?" (Asking for a credit card.) Or *"Great! Go to youngliving.com and . . ."*

This close is *fabulous* after an in-person or online class. You can talk/message just to your invitee or if you have time, each person in the class individually.

This close can also be customized for a "make and take": "Which one of these are you the most excited about using? What other oils are you interested in? Tell me more about that. Great! Here's your order form. Put your name on that line . . . tick that box for the bundle that has all those oils you want."

This close can be customized for a one-on-one presentation. "So, what part of this is resonating with you? Tell me more about that. Fantastic! Pull out your phone and let's do it!"

What makes this close so powerful is that people love to buy. They hate to be sold. In this one, you just let them talk themselves into the sale. Let me ask you a question. Write down what is true for you. At the point of sale, what percentage of your sale is emotional and what is logic?

Whatever you write down is true for you until the moment of sale. At that moment, it is 100% emotion. You can logic your way into it . . . or you can logic your way out of it. "How am I gonna 'splain this to my hubby?" But, at the *moment* of decision, it is 100% ***emotion***. If you don't feel right about it, you back away. So, when you get them talking, their own voice is talking them into it. They are selling themselves, which feels right to them.

CLOSING LIKE ERIC WORRE

The Eric Worre close is a series of questions, and it's really, really effective for a logically minded business prospect. You'll see why.

> *"What did you like best?"* Or *"What caught your attention the most?"*
>
> *"On a scale of 1-10, 10 being ready to get started, where do you see yourself?"*
>
> *"How much money would you need to make, on a part time basis, to make this worth your while?"* (Sample answer - $500)
>
> *"How many hours a week are you able to work to get you that $500?"* (Sample answer – 20)
>
> *"How long would you be willing to give me to earn to five hundred dollars a month? 6 months?"*

> If I, would you . . . *"If I could show you how to get to $500 a month, working 20 hours a week, over the next 6 months, is there anything else you need to know to get started?"*

And then . . . ZIP IT . . . ZIP. ZIP. ZIPPPP IT! **Anything you say after the close is only talking people out of the close.**

CLOSING LIKE MARCELLA - THE "YES" CLOSE

Marcella taught me this one too. The idea is to get people used to saying "yes." "If you get three yeses, you have people's attention. If you get five, you have them hypnotized." When she said that, I memorized it.

> *"Can you see the harm the chemicals we're using is doing to our families?"*
> *"Can you see yourself using these plant-based solutions on yourself and your family?"*
> *"Can you imagine life with empowered hands and no child proof locks?"*
> *"Are you ready to kick the chemicals to the curb?"*
> *"Do you want to know the best way to get them?"*

Then you can follow up with the presumptive close.

THE PRESUMPTIVE CLOSE

The presumptive close is kind of a subset of other closes. The idea is to intentionally assume your friend is "in." If you're doing it after the person has said, "No," then it's manipulative and icky. But if you're in a really great conversation and the buyer has demonstrated the right buying signals, you can say:

> *"The way we do this is to pull out your phone . . ."*
> *"Go ahead and use this computer . . ."*

"The next step is to get these oils on you and see how your body likes them! How would you like to take care of this?"

Some prefer to have everyone whip out their phones and sign up on the spot. This demystifies the process, so they see how easy it is to share with their neighbor or mama or friend.

"The way we do this is so easy! Pull your phones out. Go to www.youngliving.com and click 'Shop.' "

Or,

If you are using forms, *"Here's the form to fill out. Put your name and address there. Tick the box for the bundle you want, unless you want all four."* (Don't laugh. People do that.)

THE BEST/WANT TO CLOSE

This is a variation on the Presumptive Close.

"The best thing to do is click "subscribe and save" so you unlock the 24%."

Or,

"You'll want to order 100 PV so you lock in the 24% discount for a year."

CHOICES CLOSE

"You can get those 3 oils for $140.13, which does unlock the 24% off or you can buy the whole set of 12 oils including the diffuser for $165. That's 9 more oils for $25 plus a free diffuser. Which way do you want to go?"

Or,

"Sure! You can just order those two oils, and if you put one on subscribe to save, you'll unlock the 24% as long as you have something on Subscribe to Save. But if you add that bottle of Progessence Plus™ you were talking about, that will be enough to unlock the 24% off for a year. It's your call."

The answer is obvious to most. This is an excellent close whether you're at farmer's markets and trade shows or at the swim meet talking to a friend. You've just talked about Frankincense, Panaway®, Valor®, and Peppermint and importance of a diffuser. Run the numbers and present the options.

GOOD, BETTER, BEST CLOSE

A variation on the Choices Close.

"A great way to grab your oils is to buy those oils we talked about for $121 which unlocks the 24% for a year. A better idea is to put it on Subscribe to Save so you earn 10% back. The best thing to do is to think about that wish list and order it at the same time because you receive $159 in gifts with your purchase!"

THE THREE PRICE- POINT CLOSE

Another variation on the Choices Close

"You can grab the Professional Brand Partner starter bundle for $XXXX, which includes the Premier Aroma™ Collection and the Brand Partner package. That kit will take a year off your product learning curve. Then, you'll

have all the oils for your personal use and demonstration, and you can be free to just buy NingXia Red®, Thieves® stuff, and supplements for a while."

Or

"You can snag the ELITE STARTER BUNDLE including a set of oils + diffuser, NingXia Red® Loyalty Rewards, and Thieves® Household Cleaner for $XXX, which gives you $XX in FREE product plus $X in ER points!" Run the current numbers.

Or,

"you can go with the Starter Bundle for $X like we've talked about. Which one do you think is best for you?"

People often buy the middle option because they don't want to look cheap. And, once in a while, people buy the big option. I've used this regularly and successfully at vendor events to enroll people with the 300 PV option.

Now some of you are thinking, "Wait, I've never heard of a Professional Brand Partner Starter Bundle. When did that become a thing?" The answer is I made it up. I make these up all the time based upon what the prospect needs. I've got "Skinny Girl" bundles, "Mama Knows" bundles, "Cleansing" bundles, "Dudes" bundles, "Exercise" bundles, "Hormone" bundles, "Hello Gorgeous" bundles, "Biz in a Box" bundles . . . You name it. Have fun with this! I print up order forms and have them ready to go at vendor tables because, remember, people love to buy! Your bundles can include starter bundles, but they don't have to. Anything over 100 PV unlocks the 24%! It's absolutely genius!

FOMO CLOSE

This is a real gem, especially in Young Living®. FOMO stands for "fear of missing out," and it is a powerful motivator to get people to make the decision *now*. We have discussed the reasons you want someone to make the decision without hesitation. Recall that most people are battling their paradigms and lies in their head. If they think about it too long, the paradigm often wins. There are other reasons people drag their feet. Perhaps they are traveling, or juggling kids or busy at work, or have to cook dinner, or pregnant and they just don't feel like getting up and finding a credit card. FOMO gives them a reason to make the purchase a priority.

FOMO in the Young Living® environment is a consequence of being a true farming company. Products legitimately go out of stock. Seriously, have you tried gardening? If tomato season is over, can you quickly whip up more in a few days? On a side note, the fact that our products go out of stock, adds credibility to the fact that YL products are not manufactured in a lab.

FOMO also happens naturally when there is a sale or incredible gift with purchase offers that have a time limit. What you may not realize is that you don't have to wait for Young Living® have a sale or promotion to take advantage of FOMO. You can create urgency whenever the need arises. Are they a flight risk? What is the product they need most? Just create a bundle tailored for them and tell them the offer expires at the end of the day.

At a class you might say,

> *"I've got ONE bundle available. The first one who says, 'I'm in' gets to take it home! The rest*

> *of y'all get to have it shipped!"* This technique can result in a storm of people raising their hands and saying, "I'm in!!!!" Oooh, it's a beautiful sight.

At a vendor event you might say,

> *"I have a show special. Take it home now and there won't be any shipping."*

Or,

> *"I'm running a special right now through tomorrow night. Here's my link. If you get this done before then, I'll give you a bottle of* (whatever it was they loved that is allowed by Policy and Procedure) *as a thank you for changing your life!"*

Or,

> *"I've got kit in my car. It's promised to somebody else tomorrow, but if you want it today, I think I can get another one for them. So, I'd be happy to let you have it now."*

Or,

> *"This product is in stock right now, but it usually isn't. If I were you, I would run!"* #gotyourback

MONEY BACK GUARANTEE CLOSE

When I was a Senior Star, I got wind that Marcella Vonn Harting was speaking at an event within a five-hour drive of me, and I was determined to go hear her talk. I wore my brand new bright-yellow dress, bought new shoes with matching jewelry which I couldn't afford, drove the five hours through construction traffic to a place I had never been, sat in the geometric middle of the first row beside people I had never met, and took notes, copious notes. That talk changed my life. One of the jillion things I learned was this close, and I can likely do it exactly like she said it. I practiced it that much.

> *"I'll tell you what. You take these oils home. You plug in that diffuser and use it every day. You anoint yourself, anoint your friends, anoint your family, anoint your church, anoint your neighborhood. I don't care if you drink 'em. In 30 days, if you don't think they work, you give me my empty bottles back, you give me my diffuser back, and I'll cut you a check for every dime you spent, including tax and shipping. I've made that deal with hundreds of people, and nobody has ever taken me up on it."* (PAUSE) (PAUSE) (PAUSE) (PAUSE)

Take note: experts call this pause "Dynamic Silence." Back in the day, we said, **"He who talks first, 'loses'."** What is really going on is the more you talk, the more you talk them out of the sale. This technique is important to all the closes.

THE BOSSY CLOSE

Relationships are like bank accounts. Every time you care about your friend, serve your friend, and listen to your friend, you are depositing "money in the bank." When you ask favors, you are withdrawing. So, if you have enough "money in the bank" with someone because that someone is your big sister or your bestie, you can call them up and just boss 'em.

> *"I discovered a thing. You need it. Give me your credit card."*

Or,

> *"Hey. I started oils. I don't know much, but I know enough to know I'm not doin' it without you. Get it. Credit card, please."*

Or,

> *"You know me enough to know I've done my research. Here's my link. Time to enroll with my hippie oils!"*

Or,

> *"Girl, just get your kit. I'll teach you how to use it when it arrives!"*

CONSULTANT CLOSE

This puts you in the position as a consultant, searching for the best solution, and it is particularly effective when your prospect calls you because if they call you, they obviously want your opinion. You have the ability to really get to the heart of their needs and create a couture package. You can ask, "What are you hoping Young Living® will do for you?" or "What situation are you hoping to solve?" or "What is your budget?" Then, you can offer solutions.

> *"Based upon your priorities, it sounds like the way to go is to start with the Premium Starter Bundle this month and the NingXia Red® and Endoflex™ next month. How does that sound?"*

Or,

> *"OK So, it seems like helping your kids with a bedtime routine is your biggest priority. I'd recommend you start with the Premium Starter Bundle. It gives you all my favorite sleep oils so you can try them out in the diffuser to see what works the best. Then, you can order larger bottles of the oils you find yourself using. How does that sound?"*

Or,

> *"I've been taking notes as we talked. How about if I go home and put my thoughts together and*

make a bundle for you based upon what you've told me. I'll send you a link. Does that work?"

SIMPLE CLOSE

What do all these have in common??? It's just a question. **Just ask the question!**

Really, any close will do because it puts the ball in their court. It gives them the opportunity, the choice. If you don't close, **you are choosing for them.** *You* are being their "*No.*" What if someone had never closed you?

Let me tell you a story of a consummate salesman; his name was Bob. I met him back in the day while working with Thompson Consumer Electronics/RCA in rural Tennessee. I worked with the people who sat on phone calls, teaching people how to program their VCRs. WHAAA??? Yes, it was that long ago.

The call center of several hundred reps was a "cost center" (meaning it cost the company money). The company wanted to turn it into a "profit" center by selling service contracts to the people who called in. I was hired to train their "service" reps and make salesmen out of them.

The biggest hurdle people had to overcome was a mindset hurdle. Everyone wanted to be in "service" but nobody wanted to be in "sales." They didn't want to be *that* person. Sound familiar? They had to make the mental flip that if someone wants something and you know it exists, but you don't offer it, that isn't good service, is it? And so, we trained. For weeks, I ran those reps through mindset and skillset training for a product I *never* would have bought myself.

I mean, are you kidding me? Service contracts? Everyone knows those are a waste of money! *Right?* Nope. Not right. It turns out people *love* service contracts. They love the peace of mind. They love the simplicity and the ease. They love it. People were so grateful for the option.

You know the 80/20 rule, where 20% of the group does 80% of the job? Well, this was no different. Their **top** salesman was Bob. Bob had made the mental flip, and Bob, by himself, was selling nearly 80% of the service contracts with his oh-so-sophisticated technique. Here it is:

First, Bob would solve the problem and help people program the VCR. Then, Bob would casually mention to every single person,

> **Bob:** *"You know, we have service agreements on those units, you know, where you never have to worry about paying for a repair . . ."*
> **Caller:** *"oh, yeah?"*
> **Bob:** *"Yeah . . . Want one?"*

(Pausing now for that to sink in.)
That's it. "Want one?" That was the magical unicorn close that was doing the trick. There was Bob, signing up people right and left. "Want one?" So, what is our version of "Want one?"

> *"Are you ready to get started?"*
> *"Are you ready to go?"*
> *"Want to grab your bundle now?"*
> (All said with enthusiasm!)

There's a guy on my team who closes like this: He answers all the questions and then rubs his hands together excitedly with a great big grin on his face and says, "So! You in?" How simple. How pure. How fun!

I still chuckle about that. It might be my favorite close ever.

People Don't Buy Oils. They Buy YOU
So Many Opportunities Waiting
to be Harvested

Let Me SHOW YA HOW IT'S DONE

"It is better to hit the wrong note confidently than hit the right note unconfidently." ~Beethoven
"Just do it." ~Nike®

Just do it, and do it like you mean it. You only get better with practice. The Law of Growth states that he who is faithful with little is given much. You want to influence the world, but you won't influence the person standing right beside you at the checkout counter? You want to have epic sales skills, but you won't use the ones you've got? That's not how it works. So, what are you scared of?

What if they think I'm crazy?
What if they say NO?
What if they don't like me?
What if they think I'm trying to sell them something?
What if I sound stupid?

Aaaah, friend. That is fear talking, isn't it? We talked about this a little earlier. I find that there are three categories of fear that hold most people back: fear of what others think, fear of success, and fear of failure. If this is you, there are very helpful personal growth books. Pick up anything by Bob Proctor, Lisa Nichols, Les Brown, Zig Ziglar, Jim Rohn, or a host of other "personal development" authors. Just know this: The only thing to fear really is fear itself.

So, are you scared? I get it; I do. I was scared to write this book . . . *terrified actually*. The thoughts that assaulted me were unbelievably hateful. There were tears and panic attacks and sleepless nights. Oh, friend. I *get* it. But did you think that Brewster's millions were going to knock on your door, or do you understand that we must conquer our fears in order to succeed? Your current results are a picture of your personal development, so in order to receive more, you need to develop yourself more.

Joseph Campbell famously said, "The cave you fear to enter holds the treasure you seek." I chose to take that to heart, control what I was thinking about, and power through by God's grace. But that . . . is yet another book. So, are you scared? ***Do it anyway.***

I'll tell you what I think about when I'm scared. I think about who I'm serving. I think about who will benefit from my work. Think back to some of those texts you received that said, "I wanted you to be the first to know . . ." Imagine all the moms who have empowered hands and babies who are sleeping and Uber drivers that have more time with their children. **That's why we do this.**

So, can we just have a little conversation, you and me now? What did you resonate with as you read this book? Tell me more about that.

I believe the world needs Young Living®. I believe there are people praying that someone will cross paths with them in a divine appointment to offer them the solutions they have been asking for. I believe there is no better person than you to do that. If you believe what I believe, you will step outside your comfort zone and close!

Can we agree you have a moral obligation to do good and not evil to those around you? Can we agree you're better today than you were yesterday? Can we agree that if all you do is give your oils to someone, you're giving them a fish and not teaching them how to fish?

So, here's what you're gonna do. You're going to FORD everyone you meet. You're going to stay in relationship with them. You're not going to worry about perfection, but rather, concern yourself with the honing of your craft. You're going to serve.

You're going to finish the book, then call someone and say, "Hey! I just got done reading this book, and I was thinking about you. When are we having coffee?"

And the *reason* you're gonna do that is because if you don't, someone else will. And then they won't be on your team, and they might not get the education they need, and Lord help us all, it might be the corner box store that sells them, and then they're gonna use those perfumes and think oils don't work.

A good thing to do is start by learning just one close. A better thing to do is to binge watch every YouTube video you can find on closing. The best thing to do is to start teaching this to your team because, when you teach, you learn better than anyone.

I guarantee you if you use these skills, you will transform your business. You go out there and practice. Practice on your friends. Practice on your family. Practice on your neighbors. Practice on your social media friends. Practice for a year. If you don't agree that your skills have improved, you call me. Give me my book back, and I'll give you your money back from this book, including tax and shipping.

So . . . *You in?*

How Did I Get Here?

ABOUT THE AUTHOR

The truly important stuff about me is peppered throughout this book. I have bared my soul about triumphs as well as tragedies, but the main takeaway I want you to have is that you *do* have what it takes to ridiculously succeed.

I have a Bachelor of Science from Butler University. I graduated Cum Laude with a focus in education. Bla Bla Bla . . .

The rest of the story about me is that I have been married to the man of my dreams for 35 years, and we have built a life with our six boys on an 80-acre hobby farm.

My journey into natural wellness began when one of my boys was given a life altering diagnosis. After my world crumbled, I decided that I wouldn't accept his fate, and **Warrior Mom** was born. Don't worry; we changed his path, and he has a bright future ahead of him. Boy, if I had known about oils back then . . . but that story I will (you guessed it) save for another book.

This is probably where I should tell you that I like sunsets and long walks on the beach, but the reality is I am likely to be found puttering around the farm, weeding my garden, homeschooling my kids, or answering questions about natural birth and nursing. (Young moms, listen to those who have been there, just sayin.')

"No thanks," for the chocolate, but if you have cookie dough on you, I can smell it, and it will likely be confiscated and devoured in the closet, and I will absolutely blame it on the cats and dog. Sorry, not sorry.

If you ever find yourself on my doorstep, you might be pulled into a quilting circle or find yourself swing dancing with my boys or watching me tango with my husband.

I believe I was put in your path for a reason and now that you have gleaned from my experience, I want you to go out and conquer the world. Seriously, put the book down, drink your NingXia Red®, Valor® up, and go do the things.

A Typical Day at the Borre Farm

That's What People Say
(Reviews)

As a writer, I appreciate the tremendous amount of work that went into creating a book like this—one that truly educates and guides people in building a successful Young Living® business. I was impressed by Lori's ability to inspire and motivate, as she shared her own experiences and discoveries in network marketing. Her engaging style made it fun and interesting to read.

All Brand Partners, from Star to Royal Crown Diamond, will benefit from Lori's unique approach in sharing the business with someone new. For many people, that is the most difficult moment, but Lori makes it easy and all-possible! Seize the moment!

Mary Young
Co-founder and CEO
Young Living® Essential Oils

I have had the privilege of knowing and learning from Lori for the last few years and I always leave our conversations with pages of notes and a head full of inspiration. She walks out her talk as a top, consistent enroller with our company. Lori effectively teaches brand partners how to listen thoroughly, to communicate effectively, and to walk a friend (or stranger!) right into the products they dearly need. READ THIS BOOK. Period, end of sentence. I believe it will be dog-eared, underlined, and treasured . . . and if you do what she suggests your business will thrive!

Erin Rodgers
Young Living® Royal Crown Diamond and Author

With energy, humor, and fresh inspiration, Lori Borre packages her years of knowledge, experience, and proven closings skills into this little book, leaving the reader with an important epiphany: "I really can do this thing!"

Lori Borre proves her point in *The Harvest: Service Driven Sales in a ME Driven World* by convincing us that, in a very real way, all of us are already in sales. The trick to making it "come natural" is to change our perception and attitude towards it.

She wisely points out that "If you have ever tried to convince a kid to do the dishes when it wasn't 'his day,' you are in sales." The concept of persuasion is only "slimy" if you make it all about you. If you really care about people, sales is practically a ministry!

Inspiring, informative, and practical all in one book! The perfect tool for educating and motivating any organization!

Stacy McDonald

Young Living® Royal Crown Diamond and Author

The minute I started reading your book, I knew I wanted and needed to read it till the end. It felt like you had bugged my mind and my heart with the words you had put down on paper. From truth bombs to just GOLD, not just for me but for so many on my team who I know will be blessed by your wisdom. Truth be known, I skimmed the chapters but had not gotten far as I read and re-read. Your message aside, it's your heart to serve and help many is what comes through these pages.

Teresa G. Valmonte

Young Living® Crown Diamond

I've seen Lori Borre do exactly what she teaches in this book. It wasn't weird. It wasn't awkward. Truly, Lori has a gift in communication and connection, but her brilliance goes a step further when she breaks it down into follow-able steps. What's here in this book is pure gold, soak up every word.

Bethany Shipley
Young Living® Diamond

"I read *The Harvest* today from cover to cover and I can say with all certainty that anyone building with Young Living® MUST read this book- even if you are a seasoned leader.

The messages in this book are just what people need to hear when they are looking for the words to move people from interested to an enrolled loyal member and potential builder.

The book was such a fast read, the formatting is easy on the eyes, the messages were couched with humor and the end game is success. Thank you Lori for all of your work putting this together- what a value for Team Young Living®."

Ally Raskin
Young Living® Diamond

This is the book I've been waiting six years to read and to introduce to my leaders. It not only challenges my mindset and personal development needs, it offers truly practical tips that I can use immediately. Lori's book is truly a gift to every brand partner looking for a way to get their business to the next level. I've already read it four times and look forward to all the notes I'll take the next time around. It leaves me encouraged and brave!

April Ficklin
Young Living® Platinum

In *The Harvest,* Lori put the service in selling by pulling back the curtain on the skills that can be learned to succeed and impact others for a lifetime! By underscoring the significance of mindset, belief and the self work it takes to shift paradigms both in ourselves and those we are serving she sets up any person who's willing to dig in, sow the seeds and follow up for the harvest that comes only if they step out, make an impact and learn the learnable skills to do so. A resource full of the why, the how and the self work it takes for us all to make a generational legacy starting today.

Audrea Zigler

Young Living® Silver, Social Seller, and Mindset Coach

The Harvest: Service Driven Sales in a Me Driven World will change what you think about sales and social selling forever. Lori Borre is a well seasoned voice in a field full of greed. She challenges us to approach our work from a place of service rather than a place of serving self. She delivers the message with such a fiery passion and seemingly effortless ease.

This is one of the most honest, direct, and straightforward books that you will ever read. It took guts to write it and it will take guts to read. This book provides a clear framework for developing our mastery and maximizing our impact.

This is the plan that we have been waiting for—from a guide who has lived it. People will be reading this book, and profiting from it, for a long time.

Jaclyn Long

Young Living® Executive and Social Seller

Resources

Nothing is new under the sun. Everything I know I've heard from someone else. If I said it, chances are good it was first said by one of the greats. Because of my background, I've attended so many seminars and read so many books, it would be impossible to know where I first got the idea. Here are some of the books that have influenced my thinking:

Guerrilla Multilevel Marketing by Marcella Vonn Harting
Think and Grow Rich by Napoleon Hill
The Matrixx conference by Bob Proctor
Bible Secrets by Rabbi Daniel Lapin
David Sandler Selling System
Chris Voss Teaches the Art of Negotiation by Master Class
Basi6 Coaching Course by Melissa Poepping
Life Mentoring School by Edie Wadsworth
Gary Young World Leader In Essential Oils by Mary Young

Made in the USA
Monee, IL
03 June 2022